DARTMOOR

WALKS FOR MOTORISTS

Brian Le Messurier

30 Walks with sketch maps

COUNTRYSIDE BOOKS
NEWBURY, BERKSHIRE

*Countryside Books' walking guides cover most areas of England
and include the following series:*

Pub Walks
Village Walks
Teashop Walks
Exploring Long Distance Paths

*A complete list is available at
www.countrysidebooks.co.uk*

Originally published by Frederick Warne Ltd
This edition published 1991
Revised and reprinted 1993, 1994, 1998, 2004

COUNTRYSIDE BOOKS
3 Catherine Road
Newbury, Berkshire

ISBN 1 85306 125 5

Cover photograph of the River Taw at Small Brook Foot,
with a parish boundary stone for Belstone, South Tawton and Lydford
taken by Ken Nott.

Publisher's Note
At the time of publication all footpaths used in these walks were designated as official footpaths or rights of way, but it should be borne in mind that diversion orders may be made from time to time.
Although every care has been taken in the preparation of this Guide, neither the Author nor the Publisher can accept responsibility for those who stray from the Rights of Way.

Produced through MRM Associates Ltd., Reading
Printed by J.W. Arrowsmith Ltd., Bristol

Contents

DARTMOOR

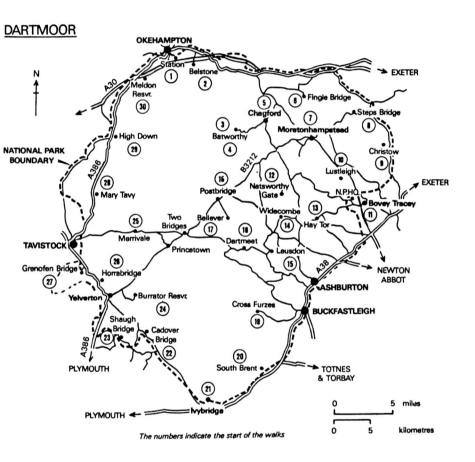

N

OKEHAMPTON

Station ①

Belstone ②

A30

Meldon Resvr. ㉚

EXETER

⑤ Chagford

⑥ Fingle Bridge

Steps Bridge

NATIONAL PARK BOUNDARY

High Down ㉙

③ Batworthy ④

⑦ Moretonhampstead

Christow ⑨

A386

B3212

⑩ Lustleigh

⑫ Natsworthy Gate

Mary Tavy ㉘

⑯ Postbridge

N.P.H.Q.

Bovey Tracey ⑪

EXETER

㉕ Two Bridges

Bellever ⑰

Widecombe

⑬

⑭ Hay Tor

Merrivale

Princetown

⑱ Dartmeet

TAVISTOCK

Leusdon

㉖ Horrabridge

⑮

A38

NEWTON ABBOT

Grenofen Bridge ㉗

Yelverton

Burrator Resvr.

㉔

Cross Furzes

ASHBURTON

BUCKFASTLEIGH

Shaugh Bridge ㉓

Cadover Bridge ㉒

⑲

A386

PLYMOUTH

⑳ South Brent

TOTNES & TORBAY

㉑

PLYMOUTH

Ivybridge

The numbers indicate the start of the walks

0   5 miles

0   5 kilometres

Introduction

It is not my intention in these introductory pages to give a history or description of Dartmoor. There are plenty of books available which provide that sort of information. However, certain features which may be new to the reader are mentioned in the walk descriptions, and it seems preferable to deal with them here rather than to define, say, the ruins of a prehistoric hut in perhaps five separate places in the book.

I also feel that the public concept of National Parks is so hazy that a few words on that aspect are required, particularly in relation to Dartmoor.

Lastly, although the form of the walk descriptions could hardly be more simple, some advice on their layout and the conventions used will help the reader derive most enjoyment from them.

The elements of Dartmoor which are particularly its own are the granite rock and the prehistoric remains. To these must be added the feeling of freedom induced by the atmosphere of wilderness on the open moor when all traces of modern civilisation are left behind.

This concept of wilderness can sometimes be heightened by the ruined relics of prehistoric man, through a sense of desertion and abandonment, and nowhere else in Britain can you find these remains so thickly grouped. In places, and Merrivale (Walk 25) is one, the low walls of his huts are clustered together among the natural boulders of the moor so that the casual stranger may not recognise them for what they are. It is the enduring quality of the rock and the lack of any large-scale subsequent disturbance which have allowed so many antiquities to be preserved.

The granite manifests itself to the visitor most prominently in the tors, a name derived from the same root which has given us the word 'tower'. Often they are hilltop excrescences, but they come in numerous shapes and situations, and are sometimes found as hillside crags and outcrops. Some of them are not granite, for where the metamorphic rock is exposed on the fringes of the moor, tors occur of that border stone. Leigh Tor (Walk 15) and the Sourton Tors (Walk 30) are examples.

I have lost count of the times I have arrived at Combestone Tor (Walk 18) with a party of strangers to the moor and been asked, 'Is it man-made?' Having replied that it is natural, the next question, 'How are tors formed then?' is asked more easily than it is answered; even the experts cannot agree! But some facts are conceded by everyone.

Granite is an igneous rock — that is, it was formed by the cooling of an upthrust of molten magma from within the earth. The magma was forced up against an overlay of rocks which have since been completely eroded by the natural elements: winds, rain and frost, over something like 290,000,000 years.

Not only has the overlay been totally denuded, but the granite has itself been broken and shattered by the extremes of climate over millions of years. This has caused the litter of rocks — the name 'clitter' which is given to them is particularly apt — on so many slopes below the tors. One theory suggests that before the rocks were exposed they were subjected to the chemical action of water circulating through the joints and weaknesses of the blocks.

Another theory is more straightforward and supposes that the tors are the remnants of the hilltop when all around has been fractured and eroded. The most easily-understood explanation of the origin of tors is to be found in the well-illustrated official guide to the *Dartmoor National Park* (John Weir, editor, Webb & Bower, 1987).

On the tor summits will often be found round hollows — rock basins, they are called — of such regular shape as to suggest a human origin. (Even between the wars the Ordnance Survey were showing rock basins on their maps in a Gothic typeface.) However, they are entirely natural, and owe their formation to the action of climatic forces on the crystalline character of the granite. The process probably begins with a large felspar crystal breaking up and leaving a hole which gets larger as the wind blows the granules round and round. Frost, ice, rain, wind and millions of years do the rest.

Prehistoric remains dating from the Bronze Age, say from 2500 BC to 750 BC, are especially plentiful on Dartmoor, but too much reliance should not be put on exact dates. They can best be divided into settlement and ritual sites.

The settlement sites most commonly found are the ruined stone walls of the circular huts — they are called hut circles on Ordnance Survey maps. The earliest date from about 2000 BC and overlap into the Iron Age, some being occupied up to about 50 BC. Mostly they occur in groups, and may be enclosed within a wall as at Grimspound (Walk 12). The huts had pointed conical roofs of some sort of thatch supported on wooden rafters. A gap in the wall for the door on the south side can sometimes be seen. Over 2000 huts have been identified, but many have been destroyed by later wall builders and field clearers. Any attempt to guess a prehistoric population is bound to fail. We do not know if the tribes or family groups were settled or nomadic, but towards the end of the period they became less pastoral and more inclined to cultivate crops. They were peaceful people.

In recent years an extensive web of field and territorial boundaries has been discovered and plotted. They take the form of earth and stone banks and are called reaves on Dartmoor. You will see one of the best of these patterns from Combestone Tor (Walk 18) which has taken the deep valley of the Dart in its stride. Another field system can be seen on the slopes of Kes Tor (Walks 3 and 4).

Iron Age hillforts with earthworks suggest tribal warfare and a breaking down of the former peaceful way of life. There are examples round the fringe of the moor at Cranbrook Castle and the Dewerstone (Walks 7 and 23).

The ritual sites can be subdivided into burial and worship sites. Barrows and cairns are common and are heaps of earth (barrows) or stone (cairns) over a burial. Sometimes the barrow has been worn or dug away, leaving only the burial chamber, a stone-sided receptacle looking like a large matchbox. The stone lid has usually been displaced. These are cists, kists or kistvaens.

Associated with these kinds of burials are the mysterious stone rows. These are single, double or triple lines of stones set on end, running in roughly straight lines over various distances. These can vary between the length of a cricket pitch, and the longest stone row in the world in the Erme valley — over 2 miles. No one knows what they were erected for. As processional ways to the burial of a chief, perhaps? (See Walks 4 and 25.)

Menhirs, or standing stones, are often found with stone rows (see Walks 4 and 25). Lastly, there are the worship sites, circles of standing stones which may have been some sort of temple — a kind of mini-Stonehenge (see Walks 3 and 25).

No evidence has come to light to show that prehistoric man cut or shaped the stones he used in his buildings or monuments. He simply used the material lying about on the surface — moorstone, it is usually called. With better tools and greater skill his successors have used the native rock to good effect to produce a wealth of interest from this intractable stone, and many artefacts will be noticed in the various walks. Besides stone buildings, look out for clapper bridges, direction posts, stiles, crosses, troughs, slotted gateposts, mould stones and edge-runners. An edge-runner is a large stone wheel which was walked round a massive stone trough by a horse to crush apples for cider, to grind bark for the tanneries and to crush young green gorse for animal feed; gorse is rich in minerals. The walls of Dartmoor are worth a close study; some are ramshackle affairs which threaten to fall down if you as much as touch them, but somehow manage to stay up, while others are more robust and a pleasure to look at. Fortunately, there are still men on the moor capable of building a good wall.

If you want to know more about these features you cannot do better than buy *The Archaeology of Dartmoor*, which was written by a professional archaeologist with a feel for his subject. It is published by the Dartmoor National Park Authority and is quite cheap. You will find the chronological chart of the different types of site very useful.

This booklet is one of the publications produced by the Authority as part of its interpretive service. Dartmoor was created one of the ten British National Parks in 1951 (eleven if one counts the similarly constituted Broads Authority), a designation which in England and Wales is a planning term, placing these areas at the top of the landscape hierarchy.

From April 1997, a free-standing Dartmoor National Park Authority is responsible for the planning and management of the Dartmoor National Park. The National Park Authority's functions are almost the same as those of the former Dartmoor National Park Committee of Devon County Council which it has replaced.

In Britain, unlike the USA, all National Park land is in private ownership. The term National Park can be misleading. It is not 'nationalised' or a 'park' in the accepted sense. Hundreds of small landowners, the Forestry Commission, South West Water PLC, the

National Trust and the Duchy of Cornwall all have a stake in the Park. So what about the open moorland? It must belong to someone.

Yes, it does, to dozens of different owners, and much of it is common land, which is an ancient term to describe land owned by one person over which others have certain rights. These rights are usually to graze animals, to dig peat for fuel, to take heather for thatching and stone and sand to repair houses. They only go with certain properties on the moor and do not entitle anyone to take what he likes. It is only common land to the commoners. However, since the passing of the Dartmoor Commons Act in 1985 the public has a legal right of access on foot to most of Dartmoor's common land, subject to certain behaviour and the observance of common sense byelaws. Another part of the Act ensures that the commoners use the land properly. A Commoners' Council adjudicates that part of the legislation.

Public rights of way, which may be footpaths or bridleways, cross the moor and thread their way through the enclosed country. These are maintained by National Park rangers with voluntary labour to assist them. They erect signposts, build stiles, clear fallen trees and apply coloured waymarks to gateposts and tree trunks to help the walker.

Other ways the National Park Authority helps the public are through the provision of information centres, a programme of guided walks and the special Dartmoor bus services. Information can be obtained from: The Information Officer, Dartmoor National Park Office, Parke, Haytor Road, Bovey Tracey, Devon, TQ13 9JQ. Tel: (01626) 832093. The annual free publication *The Dartmoor Visitor* is worth asking for.

In the summer of 1993 the National Park Authority's High Moorland Visitor Centre opened to the public in Princetown. The exhibits give a comprehensive overview of all that Dartmoor has to offer. The centre is in the splendid building which was formerly the Duchy Hotel, and is open all year except on 24th, 25th and 26th December.

Dartmoor is no museum. Farming, both lowland and hill-farming, is carried on in the traditional way, and in certain places like Ashburton, Buckfastleigh and Moretonhampstead there are small industries. It is a dynamic place, with things changing all the time, despite the feeling of communion with former ages which is so strong.

Footpaths also change. Here and there over the years the route of paths may be improved, so be ready for the occasional difficulty. Usually these will be well signposted so as to get the walker round the problem.

Dartmoor is roughly round, so the 30 walks in this book are taken in clockwise order starting from Okehampton. They all start from places where cars can be parked. You should read each walk description first for maximum enjoyment. Otherwise, how would you know that a torch is useful, though not necessary, for Walks 3 and 4? The usual descriptive convention has been followed for river banks. The left bank and right bank are always the left bank and right bank looking downstream.

Each walk description has the six figure Ordnance Survey grid reference of the starting point at the top, and all the walks are on the double-sided 2½in Ordnance Survey Dartmoor Outdoor Leisure Map, except parts of Walks 9, 11 and 27. The sketch maps, which are not strictly to scale, should be adequate for finding your way on the walk, but OS maps will tell you what you see on either side, which the sketch maps will not.

What else should you have with you? This will clearly depend on the time of year, the weather and the length of the walk, but wear comfortable clothes and especially sensible footwear. Boots are best, but it's quite possible to do Walks 14 and 24 in shoes. A waterproof is advisable. Whether you take food and drink will depend on the time you intend to take over the walk, and the availability of refreshments on the route. Where this is possible, it is stated in the walk description.

Certain walks have a warning that you should be accomplished in map and compass work if you intend to follow them in misty conditions. This is no conventional warning, but heart-felt advice not to get yourself into a dangerous situation. If the worst happens and a member of the group is lost or injured, someone should get to a telephone, dial 999 and ask for the police. There is a Dartmoor Rescue Group, which is called out by the police. If you are on your own when something goes wrong, let us hope that someone knows where you are! It is a good idea to leave a message before setting out.

Parts of the northern moor are used by the Army as a gunnery range. None of the walks in this book enters this area, but if necessary you can get details of the firing programme from Dartmoor National Park information centres, post offices, police stations and hotels in the Dartmoor area, or by telephoning Plymouth (01752) 501478.

These cautionary words are not meant to deter you from setting off, but to ensure that you are ready for the worst that Dartmoor can throw at you. Properly prepared, you will enjoy your walks to the full. And may I ask please that you observe the Country Code?

Enjoy the countryside and respect its life and work.
Guard against all risk of fire.
Keep to public paths across farmland.
Use gates and stiles to cross fences, hedges and walls.
Leave livestock, crops and machinery alone.
Protect wildlife, plants and trees.
Make no unnecessary noise.
Fasten all gates.
Keep your dogs under close control.
Do not feed the ponies.
Take your litter home.
Help to keep all water clean.
Take special care on country roads.

Brian Le Messurier

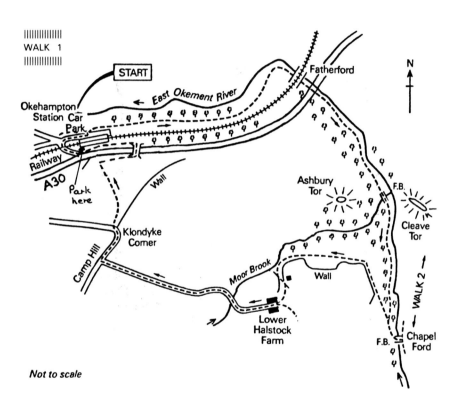

WALK 1

START

N

East Okement River

Fatherford

Okehampton Station Car Park

Railway

A30

Park here

Wall

Klondyke Corner

Camp Hill

Ashbury Tor

F.B.

Cleave Tor

Moor Brook

Wall

WALK 2

Lower Halstock Farm

F.B.

Chapel Ford

Not to scale

THE EAST OKEMENT VALLEY

WALK 1

★

3½ miles (5.5 km)

Dartmoor Outdoor Leisure Map (Ordnance Survey)

The first half of this walk from the edge of Okehampton is in the wooded East Okement valley, and there are a couple of places where a short steep climb is unavoidable. If the East Okement is in flood the path south of Fatherford may be under water, so this walk is best avoided then.

Okehampton is tucked away under the northern slopes of Dartmoor, and as it straddles the East and West Okement valleys there is a choice of approach routes to the moor for anyone staying in the town. (Grid reference: 592 944).

Leave your car on the south side of Okehampton station, which is on the higher, moorland side of the town. Turn up George Street opposite the town hall, and then up Station Road. Pass under the railway by Klondyke Road, then left into an area signposted 'Parking for Dartmoor'. The Youth Hostel in the old engine shed was opened in July 1997. The station itself is open, at the times advertised, as a visitor centre, with shops and a cafe, with weekend seasonal trains, and the service is likely to improve as the idea catches on of trains once more – after 30 years – to Okehampton from Crediton and Exeter. Tel: 01837 55330.

From the car park walk back under the railway bridge and carry on down the hill a few yards, taking a signposted level track opposite the coal yard, and just below the entrance to the station yard. (If the station gates are open you can go up to the restored station buildings before setting off, and join the track by walking down the steps opposite the station entrance.) The level track is a long-disused quarry tramway. Turn right and follow it for ¾ mile, bearing right and passing beneath the Fatherford railway viaduct and then the Fatherford road bridge. The railway is no longer open for passenger trains, but freight trains take stone ballast from Meldon quarry (to the west of Okehampton) all over southern England. The road bridge carries the A30 through the Dartmoor National Park to bypass Okehampton and was opened in July 1988. Conservation interests would have preferred the road routed to the north of the town and away from the National Park.

The path now runs into oak woodlands past the quarry (right), the source of the material for which the tramway was built. These woodlands were severely damaged in the storms of the 1980s and 1990s, but replanting is taking effect.

About 800yd south of Fatherford the path crosses the Moor Brook by a footbridge and continues up the main river past a series of cataracts. Pools beneath the waterfalls may tempt the walker to take a dip on a warm day. The path becomes steep and the Dartmoor National Park ranger service has thoughtfully provided a handrail at one point. After this section the path levels out and drops to Chapel Ford 700yd from the Moor Brook. Here there is a footbridge across the East Okement as well as stepping stones and a ford. Wild mink are sometimes seen at this spot. (Walk 2 passes here.)

Now retrace your steps for 150yd to a path junction on the slope and take the higher path, instead of the valley path you came along. This is a steep climb through the woods, but is fairly short. When the path reaches a wall at the top and leaves the woods, follow the path round to the west, contouring the hillside. Stop to admire the view across the well-wooded Moor Brook valley to Ashbury Tor on the facing hilltop.

Now make for the wall corner ahead, bear left and up a lane leading to an open space just outside Lower Halstock farm. Pass through the gate and the farmyard and take the farm road to the top of Camp Hill.

Along here you will see the Okehampton military camp over to your left. The Army began to use Dartmoor for training in the 1870s, and are firmly entrenched on the northern moor, where they fire live ammunition, explode demolition charges, fly helicopters and engage in many kinds of less destructive training. The boundaries of the firing areas are marked by red and white poles, and walkers must on no account enter a firing area when live ammunition is being used. At these times red flags are flown from flagpoles in the vicinity.

Turn right when you reach Camp Hill, admire the view to the north-west, and go down as far as the hairpin bend, Klondyke Corner. Now enter the lower of two gates and follow the well-defined path which curves away from the tree-topped wall. The fencing of the A30 now deflects the walker right for 100yd to cross the dual carriageway by a footbridge. On the north side follow the path west, then down the private road over which a public right of way exists for pedestrians, to reach the car park just before the railway arch.

12

CHAPEL FORD AND
THE BELSTONE TORS

WALK 2

★

4 miles (6.5 km)

Dartmoor Outdoor Leisure Map (Ordnance Survey)

This is an exhilarating walk along a rocky hilltop after visiting the East Okement valley. Not much fun in mist: you won't see anything!

To get to the start of the walk at Belstone, turn south off the A30 dual carriageway at the Okehampton turn-off to the east of the town. Belstone is 1 mile away. Cars may be parked in the village, but the best place is opposite the parish hall, on Brenamoor Common, beside the approach to the village from the north.

Belstone stands high between the rivers Taw and East Okement, and is built round several small village greens, on one of which stands the stocks and the pound, now a small garden. (Grid reference: 621 938.)

Leave Belstone by a road at the top of the village signposted 'Okehampton indirect'. Follow it for ½ mile to a lane on the left just past Cleave House. (Ignore an earlier signposted lane.) Turn in here; it is signposted 'Footpath to West Cleave, East Okement valley and the Moor'. The lane is short and ends at a gate with a stretch of smooth turf beyond.

The route ascends a low rise, and a rocky outcrop will be seen, right, on the crest of the valley slope. This is Cleave Tor, or the Coronet of Rocks as it is sometimes called. It is not a granite tor, but is of metamorphic rock which is found round the edge of the moor. Rock scrambling is sometimes carried on here.

There is a fine view. Beneath is the East Okement valley, where the oak woods still show the storm damage of the 1980s and early 1990s. The two Fatherford viaducts, railway and road, cross the valley ¾ mile away. Exmoor may be a blue blur to the north if the day is clear. The tors to the south will be followed later in the walk, and the track ascending Winter Tor can be picked out from here. To the west is Okehampton military camp. (See under Walk 1.)

Now return to the track and follow it south along the hillside. Just past an iron seat against the wall the track forks. Take the lower option which leads down to Chapel Ford (visited from the other direction in Walk 1) where there is a footbridge, stepping stones and a ford. Continue upstream with the East Okement river on your right, pass through a hedge gap and start to climb the hill on a path in line with the distant tor summits, your ultimate destination.

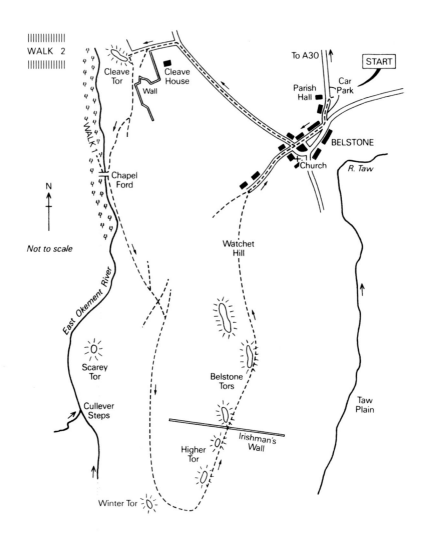

WALK 1

To A30

START

Cleave
Tor

Cleave
House

Wall

Parish
Hall

Car
Park

BELSTONE

N

Chapel
Ford

Church

R. Taw

Not to scale

East Okement River

Watchet
Hill

Scarey
Tor

Belstone
Tors

Taw
Plain

Cullever
Steps

Irishman's
Wall

Higher
Tor

Winter Tor

As the path climbs, anyone interested in plants should look to the right to see the wet seepages and their associated bog plants. One in particular is a copious spring even in drought conditions. The bright green is sphagnum moss, a plant which turns brown when dry.

The present path merges with a track coming up from the left and soon crosses the major track from Belstone (left) to Cullever Steps (right). Some 80yd beyond this track turn right along a lesser, but none the less ancient track which was made by the peat cutters bringing back fuel to their homes from the high moor.

14

The aiming point is now Winter Tor on the hillside ⅔ mile ahead and due south, and the track leads to its higher side. Carry on up to the top of the ridge, and on the watershed turn left and walk up the spine of this feature past Higher Tor to the crest of the ridge where the several summits of the Belstone Tors prod the sky. To the east is the great bowl of Taw Plain (Taw Marsh on the maps) and beyond is the massive border height of Cosdon. For many years the Ordnance Survey mistakenly called this hill 'Cawsand', but quite recently it received its true appellation. Continue along the ridge, picking your way through the boulders. Passing over this hilltop and taking a general east to west course you will see the tumbled ruins of a wall. This is known as Irishman's Wall, after a citizen of that country who had acquisitive designs on part of the moor hereabouts and sought to enclose it. He employed a gang of his fellows who built a considerable length of wall. The local inhabitants stood back, but when the project was far advanced they met in strength and threw portions of the wall over, rendering it useless. The Irishman gave up and left the neighbourhood.

Eventually you drop down the north slope to Watchet Hill with its army flagpole. Numerous old stonecutters' tracks lead across here to Belstone. A hundred and more years ago Belstone granite was much used for building, gateposts, feeding troughs and so on. The stone was roughly cut on the moor where it lay and finished off in Belstone where life was carried on to the ring of iron on stone.

The road is met at Watchet Hill Gate, and a steep drop leads quickly back to the village.

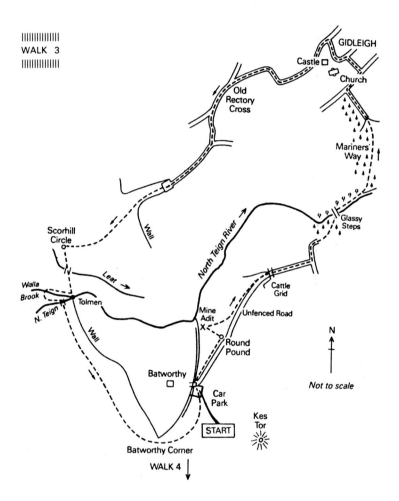

||||||||||||
WALK 3
||||||||||||

GIDLEIGH

Castle □

Church

Old
Rectory
Cross

Mariners'
Way

North Teign River

Glassy
Steps

Scorhill
Circle

Wall

Leat

Walla
Brook

N. Teign

Tolmen

Cattle
Grid

Unfenced Road

Mine
Adit
X

Round
Pound

Wall

N

Not to scale

Batworthy
□

Car
Park

Kes
Tor

START

Batworthy Corner

WALK 4 ↓

GIDLEIGH AND GIDLEIGH COMMON

WALK 3

★

4 miles (6.5km)

Dartmoor Outdoor Leisure Map (Ordnance Survey)

This is a pleasant varied walk with some climbing. There is a stretch of open moor, so take care in mist.
The walk starts from the small car park at Batworthy-in-the-Moor. This is reached from Chagford by following the signs reading 'Kes Tor Rock'. Chagford itself is 1½ miles west of the A382 between Moretonhampstead and Whiddon Down.
Walk 4 also starts from here and could be grafted on to make a long walk if desired. (Grid reference: 662 865.)

Follow the road back to the Round Pound, which has two thorn trees growing from it and causes the road to kink. Within is a 2000-year-old hut, or rather the ruins of one. The hut would have had a conical roof with some sort of thatching. Downhill from here about 150yd is a tin mine adit dating from about 120 years ago. Water trickles out, but the tunnel is fairly short and the roof seems safe enough for a brief exploration. You may get your feet wet. A torch is useful. The mine building stands to the west of the entrance.
Return to the road and follow it over the cattle grid and downhill to the first bend. Turn left here over a stile and follow the waymarks into the forest and down to the footbridge at Glassy Steps. Here one is on the so-called Mariners' Way, which may be folklore, but suggests that this was the cross-Devon foot link between the thriving ports of Dartmouth and Bideford in medieval times.
Carry on along the left bank of the North Teign for perhaps 300yd and turn left by a signpost. After a steep climb the path levels out, leaves the plantation by a gate and soon reaches the road at a stile.
Turn right here, and left at the next turning by a large tree and a phone box. This is Gidleigh — hardly a village, rather the centre of a scattered parish, but possessing a few houses, a lovely church, a small late Norman castle, and a pound (for animal strays). Jackdaws clatter round the castle ruins, rooks croak from the trees behind, and the general atmosphere has a timelessness it is hard to discover elsewhere. There used to be a Youth Hostel here, but it closed some years ago.
At the junction just past the pound (right) turn up steeply left, and the hill soon levels out into a delightful lane. Look out for slotted gateposts along this lane, particularly on the left after the second sharp corner.

17

Field security relied on separate poles wedged in the grooves rather than a hinged gate. They are probably about 200 years old.

Bear left at Old Rectory Cross, keep left at the 'No Through Road' sign, and right at the T-junction, and this brings one up to a gate outside Scorhill House.

Walk up the funnel of open land beyond the gate aiming for the top left corner. Here follow the track over the hilltop ahead and slightly left. Pause on the summit to take in the view if the day is clear. Exmoor is in the far distance behind; Cosdon is the large round hill to the north; Steeperton Tor is the hill with a prominent hut; Wild Tor spreads itself along the skyline, as does Watern Tor which is slightly closer; Haningstone Hill is behind Watern Tor and betrays its presence with a flagpole; Kes Tor is the large lump 1 mile to the south with the remains of Iron Age fields on its slopes.

Halfway down the west side of Scorhill look out for the standing stones of Scorhill Circle 250yd away from the track light. Walk across to it. This is a Bronze Age monument, probably 4000 years old, and presumably it had some religious significance. See how some of the stones have been damaged by latterday drillers, and others were carried or dragged 30yd downhill to reinforce the nearby leat bank.

Now head directly to the foot of the Batworthy enclosure wall, crossing the leat en route. In the bed of the North Teign river here is an enormous boulder with a natural hole worn through it. This is the Tolmen. It has been shifted by a flood since lying in the position where it was worn through.

Walk upstream to a single-span clapper bridge over the Walla Brook, perhaps the most photogenic on the moor, then back towards the wall to cross the North Teign by Teign clapper. The two rivers were deepened and walled up by the medieval tin streamers to lower the water-table up-river, so as to make it easier to work the valley gravels. From here follow the Batworthy wall for $^2/_3$ mile, making your own route to avoid some wet patches, then turn the corner left and return to your car a few hundred yards downhill.

CHAGFORD COMMON AND THE MARINERS' WAY

WALK 4

★

4 miles (6.5km)

Dartmoor Outdoor Leisure Map (Ordnance Survey)

This is a varied walk among prehistoric antiquities, border tors and along old tracks. The walk should not be attempted in mist unless you are accomplished with a map and compass.
The walk starts from the small car park at Batworthy-in-the-Moor. This is reached from Chagford by following the signs reading 'Kes Tor Rock'. Chagford itself is 1½ miles west of the A382 between Moretonhampstead and Whiddon Down. Walk 3 also starts from here and could be grafted on to make a long walk if desired. (Grid reference: 662 865.)

From the small car park climb the steep bank to get your bearings, then follow the wall uphill, taking care not to be too close to it as there is an unpleasant mire from which the little stream springs.
At the corner of the wall make for an irregular line of stones to the south. This is a prehistoric stone row, a linear monument associated with a burial, as a disturbed interment site will be found at the top end of the row. Another row meets it an angle, a third carries on over the hill, and a fourth may be found over the ridge heading towards the Longstone, a 10ft-high standing stone which is in fact on the line of the row, and not a terminal point. These remains and the related cairns are not more recent than about 1400 BC. The letters incised on the Longstone stand for Gidleigh parish and Duchy of Cornwall. The Duke of Cornwall (the Prince of Wales as it happens) owns a good deal of Lydford parish, and the Longstone is a parish boundary stone for Lydford and Gidleigh parishes, and for Chagford too.
Now turn round and head for Kes Tor across flat moorland. Climb to the top — the east side has an easy route up — and take in the view. You are 1432ft above sea level. The rock pool up here is one of Dartmoor's biggest rock basins, a natural feature caused by weathering. Frequently it is filled with rocks, but I have seen it empty of debris and containing 2ft of water. Small basins will be seen elsewhere on the top, in various stages of growth.
Now head slightly east of south across the moor to Middle Tor and on in the same direction to Frenchbeer Tor. At Frenchbeer Tor turn east to where a nearby wall goes down to the road. Two hut circles will be passed on the way.

19

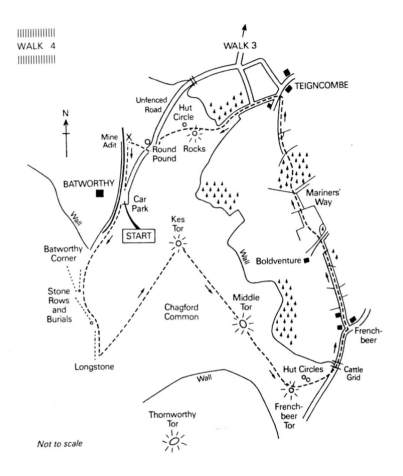

WALK 3

TEIGNCOMBE

Unfenced Road

Hut Circle

N

Mine Adit

X

Round Pound

Rocks

BATWORTHY

Car Park

Wall

Kes Tor

START

Batworthy Corner

Mariners' Way

Boldventure

Stone Rows and Burials

Chagford Common

Middle Tor

French-beer

Longstone

Wall

Hut Circles

Cattle Grid

Thornworthy Tor

French-beer Tor

Not to scale

At the cattle grid turn left and go downhill to the hamlet of Frenchbeer. At the footpath signpost turn left and follow the Mariners' Way to Teigncombe. As mentioned in Walk 3, this is possibly folklore, but a foot route across Devon from Dartmouth to Bideford has been postulated, and where it touches eastern Dartmoor it is reasonably well authenticated. This section is well maintained and waymarked by the National Park Authority. This length of the walk, from Frenchbeer to Teigncombe, is shared with the Two Moors Way, a long distance walking route from Ivybridge (south Dartmoor) to Lynmouth (Exmoor). We will come across further sections in Walks 5, 6, 12, 15 and 21.

The path follows a gated and stiled hillside track which enters Boldventure farm meadow by a stile after 400yd and leaves it opposite, entering a wet and boggy field by another stile. Some of the stiles are of the slotted variety; the bars are wedged into slots in the uprights. The wettest part of the field is provided with a boardwalk of the kind used by the forest service in Alaska. Leave this field by a gate in the far corner and head for another stile across a flat field.

The next stretch is through a plantation, at the end of which a stile gets you back into a field. From here follow another short length of boardwalk to a stile hidden in a clump of trees ahead, then follow a ditch-type stream to a pair of gates which bring you into a lane at the hamlet of Teigncombe. Here, it is said, there used to be a resthouse on the Mariners' Way.

Turn up the lane left as indicated by the signpost. It is a rough, rocky lane, almost like a dried-up watercourse. Its name is Teigncombe Common Lane. Carry straight on at a turning right, and pass out on to the open moor at a hunting gate.

Make for the top right corner of this narrowing funnel of walls — it's called a stroll on Dartmoor — and bear half right to pass beside an unnamed isolated cluster of rocks, and down to the road. You will pass a hut circle on the way.

At the road look out for the Round Pound, which has two thorn trees growing from it, and whose ruined foundations have caused the road to hiccup off course. Standing within this enclosure is the ruin of a 2000-year-old circular hut, perhaps the chief's house among this scattered settlement on the slopes of Kes Tor whose broken-down fieldbanks are all around you.

Down the slope from here in 150yd is a mine adit, a tunnel going into the hillside for 20yd or so and well worth seeing. Water trickles from its portal, but the roof appears to be sound enough to permit a brief exploration. A torch is a good idea. This was a tin mine about 120 years ago. A ruined building stands by the entrance.

From here follow the small stream back to the car park.

CHAGFORD AND
THE BANKS OF THE RIVER TEIGN

WALK 5

★

3 miles (4.8km)

Dartmoor Outdoor Leisure Map (Ordnance Survey)

This is an easy field-path and minor road walk taking in the environs of Chagford.

Chagford is $1\frac{1}{2}$ miles west of the A382 between Moretonhampstead and Whiddon Down. A large car park is signposted from the Square.

Chagford is a delightful Dartmoor border town, the inhabitants of which have been aware of its attractions as an inland holiday resort for about 120 years. There are many hotels and guest houses in the immediate area, and the shops are surprisingly good for a small town. The popularity with visitors is not surprising, bearing in mind the rich and varied scenery near at hand, and the places of historic interest awaiting discovery. In medieval times it was a stannary town (*stannum*: tin); one of the four Dartmoor towns to which tin was brought for valuation and for the paying of coinage dues. The buildings of Chagford make a harmonious group, with the church and the Three Crowns Hotel outstanding. (Grid reference: 702 874.)

From the car park, walk past the Three Crowns Hotel, across the Square and down Mill Street, forking right at the Moorlands Hotel, a 19th-century wool warehouse conversion. The road down is deeply cut through decomposed granite — growan — and the banks are buttressed with dry-stone walls and encrusted with lichen and mosses. At the bottom an attractive early-1980s dwelling on the left is a good example of a modern home in a rural setting; it stands on the site of Chagford gasworks. At the crossroads at the bottom of the hill turn right, cross Chagford Bridge and turn in at the signposted gate just beyond. From here the path is well defined and easily followed, as it is a popular local walk. It traces the river downstream without always being actually on the bank. The large building on the opposite bank was built as a woollen mill. Wool was Chagford's trade after the slump in Dartmoor tin about 1700.

After $\frac{3}{4}$ mile, as you cross a footbridge over Rushford Mill leat, the next stage is not immediately obvious. As you leave the bridge, make for a hedge gap 80yd ahead. Pass through here and make for the stile at the near end of Rushford Bridge across the field. Chagford swimming pool is 200yd along the road to the left. It is open in the summer and makes use of the disused Rushford Mill pond.

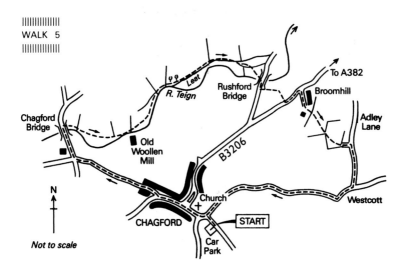

Cross Rushford Bridge, climb the stile on the south side, and walk to a stile at the far end of the field, which gets one out on to the main approach road to Chagford. Turn left here and right at Broomhill after 80yd, turning up a narrow path after 90yd which leads to a stile. Cross this, enter the field and head half right for a stile out of sight in a dip, using a white, slate-roofed house as an aiming point.

From the stile in the dip head for a tiled bungalow, and this gets one out into a short track leading to Adley Lane. Turn right here, right again at the hamlet of Westcott, and Chagford is reached after a steep end-of-walk uphill pull.

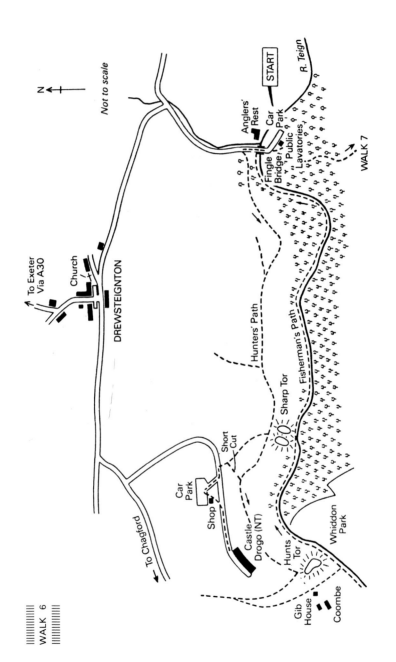

Not to scale

N

To Exeter
Via A30

Church

DREWSTEIGNTON

To Chagford

Car
Park

Shop

Castle
Drogo (NT)

Short
Cut

Hunts
Tor

Gib
House

Coombe

Whiddon
Park

Sharp Tor

Hunters' Path

Fisherman's Path

Anglers'
Rest

Fingle
Bridge

Car
Park

START

Public
Lavatories

R. Teign

WALK 7

WALK 6

FINGLE BRIDGE AND THE TEIGN GORGE

WALK 6

★

4 miles (6.5km)

Dartmoor Outdoor Leisure Map (Ordnance Survey)

This is a beautiful walk with a climb at the beginning and some rough walking later along the banks of the river Teign. There is also an opportunity to visit a 20th century castle — Castle Drogo (National Trust). The castle is open from April to October, but is closed on Tuesdays.

Park your car at Fingle Bridge, which is tucked away on the river Teign in north-east Dartmoor, 1 mile from Drewsteignton, which is itself signposted from the A382 and A30. The Anglers' Rest provides refreshment and there are public lavatories.

Fingle Bridge dates from about 1570, and has withstood enormous floods in those 434 years. The road up through the woods to the south is not recommended for ordinary cars. (Grid reference: 744 899.)

From the Anglers' Rest, walk along the road for 200yd away from the bridge, and turn up a signposted path left which climbs steeply through woods. Look out for the bulky nests of wood ants.

Where the path leaves the woods it levels out and fine views of northern Dartmoor open up, with the square snout of Castle Drogo sticking out 1 mile ahead. Approaching the tree line, the path first leaves the oak woods, then passes through a compartment of birch before entering open country past some Scots pine and mountain ash. Gorse, bracken and some heather now verge the path, known as the Hunters' Path. Fallow deer are often seen along here, regardless of the time of day, but they may have taken cover if other pedestrians are about. Look out for their white rumps as they bound away.

The craggy twin buttresses of Sharp Tor — one of ten of this name on Dartmoor — are reached. This tor is of metamorphic rock, not granite, and anyone without a head for heights should stay away from the edge. From here it is possible to turn off the Hunters' Path and visit Castle Drogo, provided it is open — see above.

If you wish to do this, walk up the path away from the tor and follow a grassy glade through the gorse; the drive leading to the castle is reached in about 400yd. Turn left here, walk to the car park and pay your admission at the shop, unless you are a National Trust member.

The building is well worth a visit, as it is the last great country house that will ever be built in England, and a granite tour de force. It was

25

constructed between 1910 and 1930 by Julius Drewe; the architect was Sir Edwin Lutyens. Of course it is a castle in name only. Lunches and teas are available, and there is a beautiful formal garden as well as acres of land around the castle.

The Hunters' Path continues on a slightly downhill course and reaches the spur of Hunts Tor, which marks the western end of the Teign Gorge. Since leaving Sharp Tor one has moved onto the Dartmoor granite. From here look across at the facing hillside, Whiddon Park. The massive wall around it, well over 6ft high, was meant to keep deer within its bounds.

At Hunts Tor walk away from the river for about 400yd, then return to the Teign along the lower path. Turn left at the river and follow this riverside path, the Fisherman's Path, back to Fingle Bridge, a distance of 2 miles. The weir below Hunts Tor provides water for the turbine house on the south bank which was part of Lutyens' project for Castle Drogo, and which generates DC electricity for the house. Much work was done on the Fisherman's Path in 1983/4 to take it above normal flooding levels, and in one place it climbs steeply for a short distance over the lower buttresses of Sharp Tor. Look out too for the foot of two scree slopes, a feature not often met with on Dartmoor.

As you near the end of the walk, look out for an inscribed boulder in the river 50yd upstream from Fingle Bridge, bearing the inscription 'Horrel 1884'. The carver was the miller at Fingle Mill, now ruinous, but still to be seen as a few dwarf walls 300yd below the bridge on the right bank. A fire destroyed the mill in 1894.

MORETONHAMPSTEAD TO CRANBROOK CASTLE

WALK 7

★

5 or 7 miles (8 or 11km)

Dartmoor Outdoor Leisure Map (Ordnance Survey)

This is a field-path and minor road walk with a considerable number of stiles — twenty-six, I think. There is a stiff hill at the beginning. Moretonhampstead is a busy little town astride the B3212 and A382. The unusual colonnaded almshouses (1637) in Cross Street are worth seeing. Leave your car in either of the two public car parks. (Grid reference: 751 860 or 754 859.)

Leave Moretonhampstead by the Chagford road (Ford Street). Nearly at the end of the built-up area, at the top of a small hill, turn right at a road signposted to Howton and after 50yd take the Butterdon fork.

Climb steadily, and after 500yd, nearly at the top of a steep section, climb a stone stile on the left (signposted) and walk diagonally across the field to a stile in the far top corner. Follow the next field edge to a third stile, and carry on beside the hedge to the fourth stile. From here the line of the path is visible ahead across a shallow valley following the hedge banks. This is a surprisingly direct cross-country route.

The next stile admits the walker to a plantation with a low row of stones picking out the path a few feet from the hedge. At the next field boundary a minor road is crossed, and the path continues beyond, again beside a plantation with the dwarf wall still present. Now leave the trees and enter a field, still with the hedge to the left, and beyond the next stile you have to cross a wet 20yd section where a small stream is crossed by a short causeway. A stile admits one to a field, followed by two more, then a patch of open moor — Butterdon — is reached.

The same general direction is followed for 300yd, when a solitary monolith (unmapped) is passed. The next stile is 100yd beyond the standing stone and admits the walker to a field. It is in fact a double stile. At the bottom of this field pass through a gate beside a disused stile and continue on the same hedge line, heading for Cranbrook farm visible ahead. Exit to the road at a stile beside the field gate and turn left.

Follow this quiet road for 400yd to a triangular road junction where there is an ancient stone direction post in the south-west corner. Turn right here, and after 100yd go left up a signposted path to Cranbrook Castle, an Iron Age hill camp with the remains of banks and ditches on its summit. A quite stupendous view opens out from here, from Exmoor in the north to Hay Tor in the south.

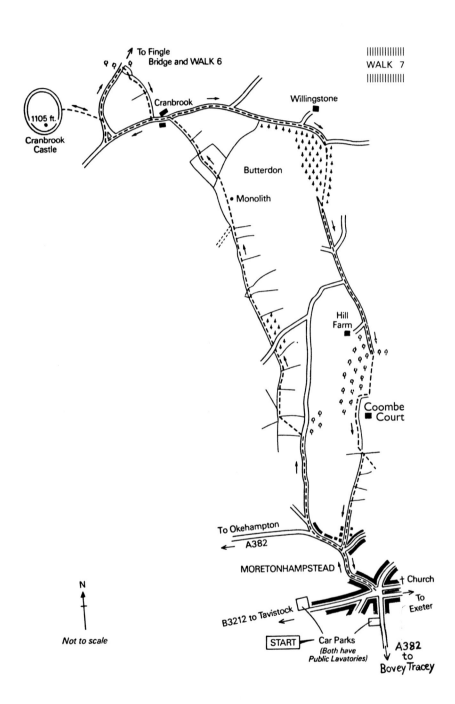

To Fingle
Bridge and WALK 6

1105 ft.

Cranbrook
Castle

Cranbrook

Willingstone

Butterdon

Monolith

Hill
Farm

Coombe
Court

To Okehampton
A382

MORETONHAMPSTEAD

Church

To
Exeter

B3212 to Tavistock

START

Car Parks
*(Both have
Public Lavatories)*

A382
to
Bovey Tracey

N

Not to scale

Return 300yd to the track and turn left to the top of the woods where a signposted path right leads back to Cranbrook farm. From this point an extension of 1 mile downhill to Fingle Bridge, plus of course 1 mile uphill back, can be made, and this links up with Walk 6. The way down and back is straightforward. There is an opportunity for refreshments at Fingle Bridge, at the Anglers' Rest.

Enter the path leading to Cranbrook farm by a good wood-and-stone stile, reflecting that none of the stone parts of these stiles are likely to be less than 200 years old. The walker will have crossed many of these today, well maintained in the traditional manner by the Dartmoor National Park ranger service. Follow the hedge left through two fields to the lane at Cranbrook farm.

Turn left here, walk along the road past the farm, right at the fork and past a large rock bearing a weathervane at the entrance to Willingstone farm. 200yd past this rock, turn in right at a signposted stile, and take the track through what was until the storm of 25 January 1990 a mature conifer plantation. After the storm more trees were lying flat than remained standing.

The route exits into a narrow lane over a stile. Walk down here to a minor road, carry straight on, and where the road turns sharp right keep going straight on along a rubble track. When the track bears right towards Hill farm, the path is now steep and rough and green and goes down towards Coombe Court. Stay on the track until the penultimate field before Coombe Court, where a 90-degree path sign directs walkers behind the farm to the right (west). Waymarks here help to identify the actual route which follows the up-slope of a hedge, and several final stiles in quick succession bring the walker down to a small valley on the outskirts of Moretonhampstead below a council estate.

A short climb, and quick stroll along a residential road, and a left turn near the hospital brings one back to the town with the feeling of having taken part in a pedestrian steeplechase!

STEPS BRIDGE TO HEL TOR

WALK 8

★

3¹/₂ miles (5.5km)

Dartmoor Outdoor Leisure Map (Ordnance Survey)

Starting and finishing in valley woodland, this walk climbs steeply to Hel Tor, a prominent border height on north-east Dartmoor.
Park your car in the public car park on the higher side of the Steps Bridge café. (Grid reference: 803 883.)

Cross the road and walk up the signposted track a few yards down the hill. Steps Bridge Youth Hostel is the wooden building up the hill to your right as you cross the stream near the road. Now walk up the narrow valley-bottom field — becoming increasingly overgrown, but I can remember when it was cultivated! — and carry on up the valley, crossing the stream once more after ¹/₄ mile. In another ¹/₄ mile enter a field by a signposted gate, and head for an oak tree by the stream which marks the crossing place of the stream yet again. Now look out for a waymarked post and path sign and a waymarked gate beyond. Pass through this gate, or climb over it should it be securely tied, and follow a lane to Burnicombe farm. Pass through the yard, and once beyond the buildings the route becomes the main farm approach and is well surfaced.

Turn right 500yd beyond the farm at the tarmaced county road, and not at the first place you become aware of Hel Tor, at a pair of gates. About 250yd along the road climb a stile on your right, and follow the permissive path to Hel Tor. Hel Tor is one of those uncommon features on Dartmoor, a tor surrounded by fields, so the National Park Authority has negotiated a fieldside path to the rock with an explanatory map and details of the access agreement on display by the stile. If walkers keep to the permitted path and tor, everyone is happy, especially the farmers, who were tormented by trespassers crossing their fields until this equitable solution was found.

From the top there is a fine view of the Dartmoor border country. The view to the west is interrupted by the foreground, but the two highest points of the moor, High Willhays and Yes Tor, can just be seen across the intervening slopes of Mardon. The summit rocks contain some of the best rock basins on Dartmoor, of many sizes. These are formed by weathering — over many thousands of years.

Now return to the road, turn right and walk straight for about ³/₄ mile. This involves turning neither left nor right at Plaston Green crossroads

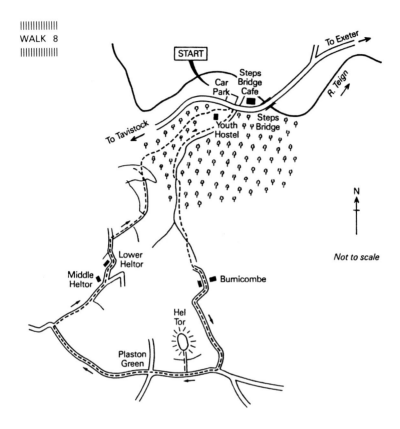

by a large beech tree. At the first sharp left bend enter a field to the right by a couple of stiles, follow the hedge/wall to the gate at the bottom, and this brings you into a lane leading to the twin farms of Middle and Lower Heltor.

From the foot of the lane go straight on through the yard of the lower of the two farms and along a lane for 150yd beyond. Turn into a field here through a waymarked gate (right), and follow the right hedge round to the gate at the end of the second field.

From here aim slightly right across a scrubby field for a ladder stile beside a gate leading into the woods. Enter the woods, turn right and follow a pleasant clear track downwards and back to the road — ½ mile. The middle section is particularly attractive as it follows the spine of a spur, with tempting half-views on either side through the thin tree cover — these views are better in winter — and with rock showing through the path floor here and there. The Youth Hostel is passed just before the road is reached.

31

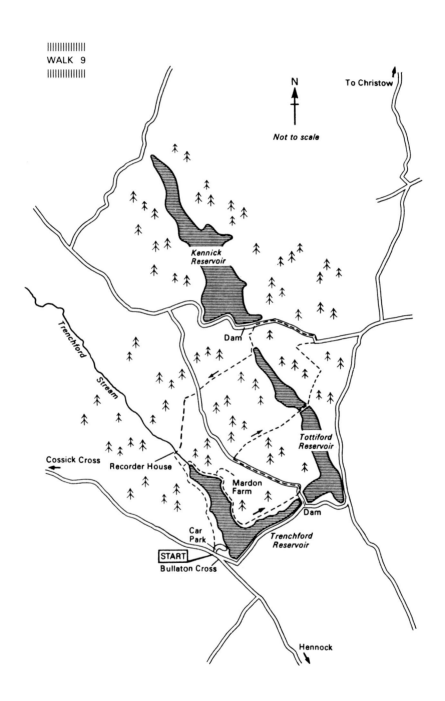

||||||||||||||
WALK 9
||||||||||||||

N

To Christow

Not to scale

Kennick
Reservoir

Trenchford Stream

Dam

Cossick Cross

Recorder House

Tottiford
Reservoir

Mardon
Farm

Dam

Car
Park

Trenchford
Reservoir

START
Bullaton Cross

Hennock

TRENCHFORD, TOTTIFORD AND KENNICK RESERVOIRS

WALK 9

★

5 miles (8km)

Dartmoor Outdoor Leisure Map (Ordnance Survey) — part only
Ordnance Survey Pathfinder Map — Sheet 1329
Ordnance Survey Explorer Map — Sheet 31

This walk touches the three tree-fringed reservoirs which occupy shallow valleys on the high plateau to the north of Bovey Tracey. It is practically all on forest paths and along the reservoir edges, and only for short unavoidable stretches are lengths of minor road included. As much of the route is through conifer plantations there is considerable shelter, so this makes it suitable as a bad-weather or out-of-season walk. Indeed, over-wintering wildfowl may be seen on the water when the human tourists have gone home. There are no steep climbs. Boots are recommended.

Walkers are warned that trees are felled when they reach maturity, so this may affect the walk description. Trees also fall during storms, sometimes in very large numbers. The storm of 25 January 1990 demolished large tracts of forest, and this circuit was impassable for about a year until clearing was completed.

The walk starts from the Bullaton Cross car park beside Trenchford reservoir (1907) and crosses Tottiford reservoir (1861), returning by the dam of Kennick reservoir (1860). The Bullaton Cross car park may be reached by following the road signposted 'Reservoirs' from the village of Hennock in the south-east corner of the Dartmoor National Park, or by taking the signposted minor road south from Cossick Cross, 2 miles east of Moretonhampstead.

The car park has an adjacent picnic site, lavatories and an information panel. The helpful leaflet available on site will give the walker additional information about the reservoirs and also shows the paths as well as additional routes through the forest.

The walk described here uses trails developed by South West Water and the Dartmoor National Park Authority. If the walker finds himself with a choice of path the correct option is the signposted or waymarked one. (Grid reference: 805 824.)

Leave the car park by the path beside the information panel. After 300yd it comes out on the bank of Trenchford reservoir. When full this is the deepest of the three — 50ft — but after a dry period a 'drawdown' exposes muddy banks and reduces the water area.

33

Follow the path round, crossing the long footbridge at the reservoir's tail, and continue along the east side. Just before the first small footbridge on this side turn sharply up left for 75yd, and at a kink in the path turn right along a less distinct path to see the ivy-covered Mardon farm ash house. This is a small round conical-roofed stone building which was used as a store for domestic ashes which were subsequently spread on the land. Ash houses are generally uncommon, but are frequently found in this circular form on eastern Dartmoor. Mardon farm was abandoned when the valley was taken over for water-gathering purposes.

Now return to the waterside path, and a short distance further on a stone building will be seen above the path on the left which has been adapted as a shelter with seats. Carry on to the gate at the end of the Tottiford reservoir dam. You will pass a pleasant mixture of oak, beech, Scots pine, rhododendrons, gorse and heather. At the gate turn left up a minor road and follow it to the end of a straight stretch, where you should climb a stile right. Follow the path within the woods, turning left where it rounds the outside of a field corner, then right after 75yd deep into the conifer plantations. The path — here called the Postman's Path — descends to a causeway built originally to prevent silt from clogging the main part of the reservoir. At the east end of the causeway bear left up through the bracken and into the plantation.

A gentle climb leads into the centre of this block of forest where you should turn 90 degrees left along a well-used path. After 300yd or so turn right and carry on to a road which you will meet at a bend. Turn left here and you will come down to the dam of Kennick reservoir. Kennick is possibly the most attractive of the three reservoirs, and is much used by anglers. Walkers are discouraged from using the banks because of the disturbance this would cause and the danger from casting.

Enter a gate at the east end and on the downstream side of the dam, noting how the overflow runs through a channel cut through the rock. The path crosses the stream at the tail of Tottiford reservoir, but after following the west bank for only 50yd, heads up into the woods again, soon following an old beech hedge right. Keep straight on to the road, ignoring paths to left and right, the road you were earlier walking along.

Cross here, and carry on down along a well-used path which twists and turns but is generally direct after an early 90 degree turn left, and the path emerges by the Trenchford Stream at the recorder hut. If you look in the window you will see the pen recorder registering the flow of the stream. Cross the footbridge here, turn left and follow the path back to the car park.

LUSTLEIGH CLEAVE

WALK 10

★

3 miles (4.8km)

Dartmoor Outdoor Leisure Map (Ordnance Survey)

This is a footpath walk through tumbled border country, with a steep climb early on.

Park your car near Lustleigh church, which is ¾ mile off the A382, 3 miles north of Bovey Tracey.

Lustleigh is an attractive village with old houses mixed up with some modern bungalows. The large pudding-shaped rocks which seem to have burst out of the ground are a feature of the locality. The church is a typical moorland sanctuary with a good 16th-century screen, and an early Christian memorial stone which for hundreds of years was used as the threshold of the church. It was moved in 1979 to prevent further wear. (Grid reference: 785 812.)

Leave the village centre by walking up past the Cleave Hotel to the parish war memorial. Turn left here, still uphill, and almost immediately left along a private unmade road (signposted). At the end of the road, beside a large house, pass through a kissing gate into a sloping field. This is the Lustleigh church path, the regular way for parishioners up the valley to reach the village centre hundreds of years ago.

Follow the upper path which contours the slope below a large rock, and at the end of the field at another kissing gate and signpost head for the bottom of the woods ahead. The course is now clear and uncomplicated until Lower Combe is reached. Turn left beside the house, taking the left track heading for the stream which is crossed by a small clapper bridge. Now turn left, then right and climb progressively steeper up a waymarked path through a woodland jungle.

A stile brings one out into the road where you turn left for 25yd, then right up a narrow lane between properties called Grove and North Park. This brings one to a gate, path junction and signpost where a left fork is taken, keeping to the wall more or less closely through attractive open woodland with many scattered rocks. From the highest point on the path you will see Sharpitor, one of Dartmoor's ten Sharp Tors, to your right. It is an idiosyncrasy of Dartmoor speech that a vowel is often inserted between consonants. Thus, Sharp Tor becomes Sharpitor; Broad Marsh and Broad Falls become Broadamarsh or Broadymarsh and Broadafalls.

This rocky eminence once bore a naturally-balanced stone famed for

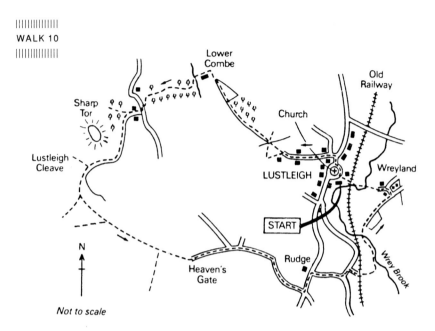

Not to scale

its ability to crack nuts, and called the Nutcracker. Unfortunately it was yanked 60ft over the edge with a crow-bar by two inebriated vandals about fifty years ago, and was damaged in the fall so that the efforts of the Royal Engineers to replace it came to naught. The name Nutcracker persists on most modern maps.

Because it is no longer grazed the character of the Cleave has changed, even in my lifetime. It used to be much more open, but before long it will be woodland, at least on the lower slopes.

Continue on and down taking Lustleigh, Pethybridge or Heaven's Gate as the next objective on signposts, which means bearing left at path junctions. You should keep left, south, and after nearly 1 mile you reach a gate. This was christened Heaven's Gate as the view across the Cleave for anyone coming out of the gate evoked feelings of paradise. But, as indicated earlier, the nature of the Cleave has changed, and trees now screen the sweep of landscape.

Pass through the gate, follow the lane to the road, turn right and walk down to Rudge Cross. Turn left here, and right opposite Rudge farm. At the foot of this lane turn left and after 30yd go right down through the demolished arch of the Moretonhampstead railway branch line (opened 1866, closed 1959).

The path now skirts the village sewage works, crosses the Wrey (or Wray) Brook by a footbridge, then bears left for 150yd before passing in front of a large boulder and climbing behind it to a gate. Follow the right field edge to another gate and into a lane leading to the beautiful hamlet of Wreyland (or Wrayland). Turn left, and the road, which degenerates into a track, leads back to Lustleigh past the cricket pitch and a brick chapel.

Anyone wanting to learn more about Wreyland and Lustleigh should read the three volumes of *Small Talk at Wreyland* by Cecil Torr, which he published between 1918 and 1923 and which were reprinted in one volume in 1970 and again in 1996. It is a delightful journey into the past; a truly relaxing bedside book.

THE LOWER BOVEY VALLEY
AND SHAP TOR

WALK 11

★

5½ miles (9km)

Dartmoor Outdoor Leisure Map (Ordnance Survey) — part only
Ordnance Survey Pathfinder Map — Sheets 1329 and 1342

This is a mixed walk of woods and field paths, with a few minor roads.
There are two steep climbs.

Park your car in either of the two public car parks in Bovey Tracey,
which stands at the crossing of the A382 and B3344, though the A382
now bypasses the town to the west.

Bovey Tracey is a lively little town, with an economy now mostly
dependent on commuters, retired people and holidaymakers. The
church is one of the finest in the Dartmoor area, with a glorious screen
and pulpit, and other interesting fittings. The Dartmoor National Park
headquarters, standing in beautiful grounds on the Hay Tor road at
Parke, was opened in the summer of 1979. The house, which is owned
by the National Trust, was built in 1828 by the Hole family, and lived in
by them until Major Hole died in 1974 aged 93. (Grid reference: 816 786
or 814 782.)

From the centre of Bovey Tracey, by the horse trough, walk behind the
Cromwell Arms and through the Cromwell Arch (a ruin of uncertain
antecedents, but older than Cromwell's day) and along a road of
Cornish Unit houses to the far end.

This is a walk with an inauspicious beginning, and it is hard to imagine
as one approaches the turning circle at the end that a narrow footway
here will take you behind and beyond the estate to a pleasant path on the
fringe of the town.

Take the cut, and turn right along a footpath, looking out for Parke,
the Dartmoor National Park headquarters, through the trees to your
left. The path is routed to cross the Bovey Tracey bypass, the A382,
which dates from 1987. On reaching a tarmac lane, turn left and pass
through the hamlet of Southbrook, following the waymarked route and
keeping to the edge of the field beyond.

You enter the woods by a stile. These are glorious beech woods, best
seen in spring or autumn, and the path is clear and direct. Another stile
is reached, giving access to a field across which the path runs to the far
end where there is another stile. The path now runs along the side of a
steep slope above the track of the disused Moretonhampstead branch

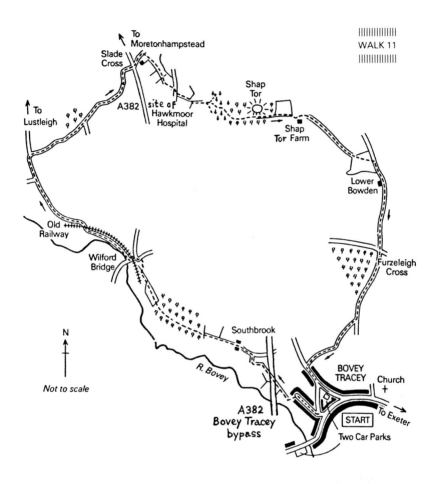

To Moretonhampstead

Slade Cross

Shap Tor

A382 site of Hawkmoor Hospital

Shap Tor Farm

To Lustleigh

Lower Bowden

Old Railway

Wilford Bridge

Furzeleigh Cross

N

Southbrook

Not to scale

R. Bovey

BOVEY TRACEY   Church +

A382 Bovey Tracey bypass

START   To Exeter

Two Car Parks

line (opened 1866, closed 1959) before briefly passing along the bottom of a field which it leaves at its foot for a steep drop down to the road near Wilford Bridge. (It is possible to trace the line of the old railway back to Bovey Tracey if time and energy — or the lack of it — demands!)

Now pass through the abutments of the old railway and turn right along the Lustleigh road for ⅔ mile. Some years ago I was told an amusing story by two elderly people who were resident in the locality in Edwardian days. The lions' cage of a travelling circus re-routed behind Parke because of drain laying in Bovey Tracey, got stuck on the bridge over the Bovey, breaking down the parapet, and frightening local folk who were alarmed to hear lions roaring in the depths of rural Devon.

Once through the overhead skewed bridge you may be able to spot the place where in the 1920s and 1930s there was for a time a stopping place on the railway called Hawkmoor Halt. This was a response to the presence of a sanatorium over the hill to the east called Hawkmoor Hospital, now closed, but was some distance from it. The hospital site is now a superior residential development.

About 270yd past a turning signposted 'Manaton' turn up right, signposted 'Nutcombe', and after 20yd take the rough track climbing left. This meets Hatherleigh Lane at the entrance to Higher Knowle nature reserve. From here follow the pleasant undulating road straight on to Slade Cross on the A382.

At Slade Cross take the Hennock road, noting the old stone direction post by the letterbox, and 80yd up the road turn in right at a footpath signpost. The path is waymarked. Pass through a gate into rough land and along the top edge of two fields but outside them at the foot of a bramble slope. Cross a stile and walk along a cinder track. It is hard to believe that the outlying buildings of Hawkmoor Hospital once stood on the slope to your right. When you reach a lane, walk down slightly and enter a field, following the bottom hedge. Pass through a gate at the end, go down a few yards and cross a stile into a field planted with a few conifers. Turn left here and pick up a track leading into the woods at the head of the valley clearing.

From the gate/stile leading into the woods, bear up right, then left, and once in the conifer plantation look out for a signpost pointing up to the right. You walk across a track and up past a brick inspection trap marked Hawkmoor Water Supply. From here on the path is clear, though steep, and soon enters Woodland Trust land.

Buzzards may be heard overhead, and around one in the woods are fenced-off shaft openings, so keep to the path. Opposite the highest point on the path to the left is a large slab of rock, Shap Tor, and a stone marks its dedication in 1988 to the distinguished naturalist, H. G. Hurrell, MA, MBE, JP. The view from the summit is magnificent and encompasses the highest points of Dartmoor. Lacking prominent summit rocks it is not a feature in the view from elsewhere, but as a place to be on a fine clear day it has no rivals, and the visitor is unlikely to have company. The skirts of the tor are bedecked with bluebells in May.

Return to the path and follow it along a green track and over stiles past Shap Tor farm. Now follow a grassy lane which leads into a field. From the gate make for the highest part of the field where a wood and stone stile leads into the road. Turn right and follow the road back to Bovey Tracey, 1 mile away.

GRIMSPOUND (FROM THE EAST) AND HAMELDON

WALK 12

★

3 miles (4.8km)

Dartmoor Outdoor Leisure Map (Ordnance Survey)

This is an open moor walk to a Bronze Age village, also visiting a Bronze Age cairn. It should not be attempted in mist unless you are accomplished in map and compass work, and in any case is best done on a clear day because of the fine views from the top of Hameldon.

Park your car by the roadside at Natsworthy Gate. This is on a little-used minor road, and it may be reached by driving either 2½ miles up the valley from Widecombe, or taking the uphill road for 1 mile from Heatree Cross. Natsworthy Gate is at the top end of a beech avenue. A signpost gives footpath and bridleway directions. (Grid reference: 721 802.)

From the gate giving access to the open moor on the west of the road follow the broad path up the hillside towards the top corner of the wall on your right. From here a prominent pointed stone becomes visible on the skyline, slightly to the left of the track. Make for it. You will find it bears the following inscription:

†

R A F

S49

RDW

CJL

RB

RLAE

21.3.41

The stone is a memorial to the crew of a Handley Page Hampden bomber, 'S' of 49 Squadron, which crashed here on its way back from operations. The names of the dead crew were Wilson, Lyon, Branes and Ellis, and the stone was erected at the request of the mother of Pilot Officer the Hon. R. D. Wilson. In the month of November I have seen it marked with small poppy-decorated wooden crosses.

Now return to the main track. (The one going up past the memorial stone will not get you to Grimspound, but bears round to head for Broad Barrow.) Carry on north-westwards, then west. The scattered poles to your left and right are another reminder of the war. They were stuck up

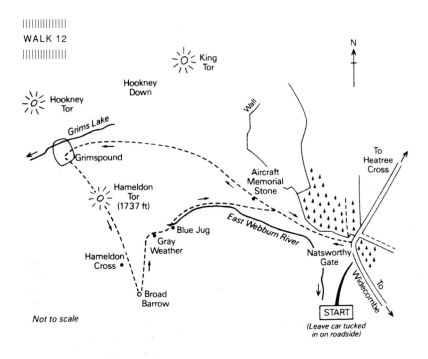

Not to scale

to deter enemy gliders from landing, and those that remain have defied sixty years of Dartmoor weather and use by animals as rubbing posts.

In clear conditions the Warren House Inn on the B3212 becomes visible as you cross the saddle south of King Tor, and as the path begins to descend the scars of mine workings come into view. This track was the mine workers' route to Manaton at weekends. During the week they lived at the mine. Look out for red grouse around here, as this is some of the best heather country on Dartmoor and they feed on heather shoots.

About 1½ miles from Natsworthy Gate the ruined wall of Grimspound is reached. It is a west-facing village site of about 4 acres with many ruined stone huts, some of which were probably stores or animals pens. The entrance to the enclosure was on the higher side, giving access to the high pastures of Hameldon, surely a clue to the economy of the inhabitants, and the indefensible site of Grimspound at a time of slings, arrows and spears, overlooked as it is, must mean that the people who lived here were peaceful folk. The wall was built to keep wild animals out and domestic animals in. The walls of some huts have been conjecturally restored. See how the stream, the Grims Lake, ran through the enclosure. However, it was not a reliable water source as it dries out in drought conditions. The site could have been occupied any time between 2000 BC and 700 BC.

From here climb the steep hill to the south to Hameldon Tor (1737ft), which is disappointing as a tor but splendid as a viewpoint, particularly to the west and north. The whole of this great hill which extends southwards for a couple of miles is referred to as Hameldon. Continue south along a slight dip, and the remains of Hameldon Cross become visible a few yards from the path right. It bears an inscription 'HC DS 1854'. The DS stands for the Duke of Somerset who owned the land in 1854 and who marked his boundary with a series of stones bearing his initials, and the names of the stones. Now head for Broad Barrow, a Bronze Age burial cairn to the south-east. This bears another DS stone, inscribed 'Broad Burrow' on its top.

From here follow a track north for 400yd to a dip in the land, and turn north-east here into a shallow depression which is the head of the East Webburn. A boundary stone, inscribed 'Gray Weather' with a grey stone beside it, is to be found at the north-west limit of rushes. The name would suggest that the stone had sometime been seen as a sheep (a wether is a castrated ram). A similar case of mistaken identity is of course the Grey Wethers stone circles near Sittaford Tor, north of Postbridge, and on the Marlborough Downs to the east of Avebury (Wiltshire) are scattered sarsen stones also called Grey Wethers. The next boundary stone, obscurely called 'Blue Jug', is further down the slope, about 200yd east-north-east.

Trace the tiny stream down, keeping about halfway up the slope. When the first trees are reached in the valley the start of the walk at Natsworthy Gate becomes visible ahead. Head for it downhill.

HAY TOR AND
THE GRANITE TRAMWAY

WALK 13

★

3 miles (4.8km)

Dartmoor Outdoor Leisure Map (Ordnance Survey)

An easy open-country walk across border moorland. Provided the weather is clear, this provides a suitable introduction to Dartmoor for newcomers.

Leave your car in the car park on the highest part of the road 4 miles west of Bovey Tracey in the south-east corner of Dartmoor. Hay Tor is signposted from Bovey Tracey. There are public lavatories at the foot of the hill. (Grid reference: 759 767.)

From the car park walk up the gentle grassy slope towards the right-hand rock of Hay Tor. You will see that from this side the lump you are aiming for is the dominant feature. From the north this influence is reversed.

Halfway to the rock from the road look out for a rock perched on a couple of small stones standing on the edge of the bracken area. Peer underneath and you will see it has been worked to a smooth surface, but presumably a fault developed and after being half completed as an edge-runner for some sort of crusher it was rejected. I wonder how many of the people who pass it realise what it is?

The tor can be climbed, but anyone with slippery footwear or lacking a head for heights is advised not to make the ascent. There is a wide gap to cross near the top and the rudimentary steps cut in the rock can be treacherous. From the summit, 1490ft, a fine view can be obtained. On a clear day you can see across to Princetown on western Dartmoor which is backed by North Hessary Tor with its BBC television mast. Exmoor may be seen as a blue blur to the north, and the Teign estuary is conspicuous in the other direction. The white scars in the valley to the east are ball clay workings. At your feet notice the large white felspar crystals which are one of the constituents of granite, the others being mica and quartz.

Now carefully descend and go down the path towards the quarry spoil tips visible to the north-east. When you reach the edge of the inner quarry you will see it contains two deep pools, and the scene is one of beauty and tranquillity. Enter the quarry by the entrance on the north-east side. A fallen derrick lies half in the water, and if you are lucky you may spot goldfish in the deeper of the two ponds. They manage to escape the depredations of visiting herons, presumably

44

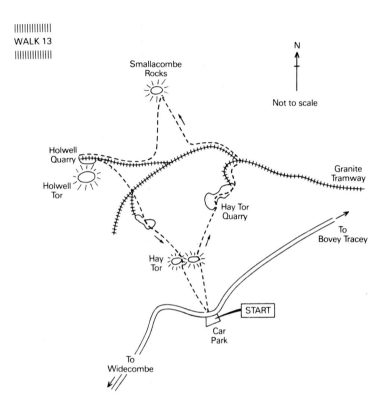

because of the depth of the water. Dragonflies skim the surface. The quarry was worked from about 1820 to 1860, and stone was sent to London for many public buildings.

Move out of the inner quarry. The outer, lower-level quarry is passed, and a cutting giving access to this one should be followed, and its track traced round to the left beneath tips of waste rock. At this point you will notice two parallel lines of grooved stone blocks like railway lines, which is what in fact they were. Keep following them away from the quarry where they bear round to the right across a broken embankment, and the quarry branch line soon meets the 'main' line at a spot where the stone blocks form a set of junction points.

This is the famous granite tramway which was used from about 1825 to 1858. Stone was loaded on to flat-top, wooden-wheeled trucks pulled by horses which took the stone 8 miles down into the valley where it was transferred to barges for conveyance to Teignmouth and loading into sea-going vessels. This double transhipment made the quarry uneconomical to work. The system reverses the normal railway technique which has the flange on the wheels and employs simple rails. Here the retaining flange was on the rails, or sets, and the material was available for the cost of extraction.

45

Follow the tramway up a slight gradient, round a gulley and into a cutting. When it comes out of the cutting and heads straight for Holwell Tor leave the tramway and head north-west across level ground for Smallacombe Rocks, a tor in all but name. It is incorrectly called Grea Tor on some maps, Grea Tor is the much larger feature halfway up on the other side of the valley. Beside Smallacombe Rocks on the east side are the ruins of several prehistoric huts.

Soak in the view from here. Hound Tor is the huge tor to the west and the Becky (Becka) Brook flows down the valley. Listen and you may hear the 'cronk cronk' of a raven, and maybe the sound of wing beats will first alert you to the presence of these large black birds.

The next place to visit is Holwell quarry whose rock face is visible across the small combe (hence the name of these rocks) to the south-west. Don't take a direct course as marshy ground intervenes; instead follow a path in line with Hay Tor, and after 300yd veer off right towards the granite tramway where it ran down to Holwell quarry. This is the haunt of the stonechat; listen for its metallic call.

As you approach the quarries a ruined blacksmith's shop is seen left, and soon the sheer vertical face of the main quarry. Past this and on the lower side of the tramway is a well-preserved workmen's shelter with its roof still intact.

Retrace your steps along the granite tramway for 150yd and mount the path to the right just before a wet section by a few rowan trees. Where this path levels out make for yet another quarry straight ahead in line with Hay Tor. This one rejoices in the name of Rubble Heap. Note how the westerly lump of Hay Tor has now achieved supremacy. Walk into the quarry, scramble up the easy path at the back and head for the larger block of Hay Tor. This part of the moor can produce masses of succulent whortleberries in August. The tor can be climbed with the aid of iron hand-holds, and is in fact higher than its more frequently climbed sibling. Now head downhill back to the car.

WIDECOMBE-IN-THE-MOOR TO THORNEYHILL LANE AND BONEHILL

WALK 14

★

3½ miles (5.5km)

Dartmoor Outdoor Leisure Map (Ordnance Survey)

This walk is mostly on quiet country roads, but with one steep rough section.

Widecombe-in-the-Moor is reached by following the signs from Bovey Tracey or by turning off the Dartmeet road at Poundsgate. Park in the village car park.

Widecombe has achieved through its fair and song the sort of fame (some might say notoriety) which few small country villages possess. Grasmere (Wordsworth), Oare (the Doones), Polperro and Castle Combe (quaintness), Stoke Poges (Gray's *Elegy*) and Selborne (Gilbert White) are other places which for literary and landscape reasons have this power to attract.

Certainly the village has a superb valley site, and the church tower is the finest on Dartmoor, drawing the eye from all points of the compass. The far-flung parish too has many features of interest for the discerning visitor: numerous old stone farms, isolated patches of moorland, valley woods, prehistoric remains, tors and rocks.

In the large church look out for the fragments of the medieval rood screen and, in the base of the tower, the rustic verses describing the great storm of 1638 when lightning struck the tower, causing some of the masonry to fall into the church, killing several worshippers.

The church house is the nearest building to the tower, and is now the parish hall. It also houses a National Trust shop and information centre. In its time — and it was built about 1550, if not before — it has been brewhouse, almshouse, poorhouse and school. The village green was once the local archery training ground. Just below the post office is the village well, but it is not advisable to use it for drinking water.

Widecombe Fair is held annually on the second Tuesday in September. A one-way traffic system operates as so many people want to come, and it really is a worthwhile experience. There are animal classes, show jumping, sideshows, stalls, a small funfair and someone dressed up as Uncle Tom Cobleigh. The young men have a race to the top of Widecombe Hill and back.

The village sign was designed by Lady Sayer, a local resident, to replace an earlier one destroyed when signs were suppressed during the war. (Grid reference: 719 769.)

47

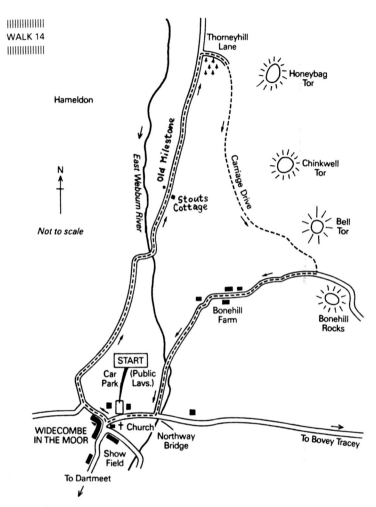

Honeybag
Tor

Chinkwell
Tor

Bell
Tor

Thorneyhill
Lane

Hameldon

N

Not to scale

East Webburn River

Old Milestone

Carriage Drive

Stouts
Cottage

Bonehill
Farm

Bonehill
Rocks

START

Car
Park

(Public
Lavs.)

WIDECOMBE
IN THE MOOR

† Church

Northway
Bridge

To Bovey Tracey

Show
Field

To Dartmeet

From the green, leave the village by the wooden tea hut and follow the road up the valley towards Natsworthy. Just past Stouts Cottage on the right look out for an inscribed stone on the left of the road bearing the legend '1 MIOL'. This was carved by a local mason as he pronounced it, and probably dates from early in the 19th century.

After 1½ miles, just before a cattle grid, turn steeply up right. This is Thorneyhill Lane, and it leads to a pleasant open level carriage drive which contours south below Honeybag Tor and Chinkwell Tor with glorious views across and down the valley.

At the next road, turn right down Bonehill, passing the fine group of Bonehill farms. At the T-junction turn right, and the village is reached in 200yd.

48

LEUSDON, DR BLACKALL'S DRIVE AND SPITCHWICK

WALK 15

★

6½ miles (10.5km)

Dartmoor Outdoor Leisure Map (Ordnance Survey)

This is a varied walk with open moor, field paths and a riverside walk. It has a not very severe climb at the end.

Leave your car on the grassy triangle near Leusdon church, Leusdon Common. To find Leusdon, turn off the Ashburton to Dartmeet road at Poundsgate along the Widecombe road, then right by a large monolith erected to mark the 1977 Silver Jubilee. (Grid reference: 708 732.)

Walk west along the wide level road below the Old School House, with the West Webburn in the valley to your right. After 900yd, turn up left through Sweaton farm and follow the lane uphill. At the top of the lane cross a stile and walk on the right side of the hedge. At the top of this field pass over a stile to the other side, continue upwards and exit to the lane by a stile.

Turn right along this minor road, then up left when the open moor is reached, keeping outside the enclosures. Make initially for a wall corner marked by a prominent thorn tree just beyond a leat running north to south, but which may be dry. Now bear slightly left and head for the next wall corner. Leave the wall at 45 degrees and you should reach the main road at Bel Tor Corner where there is a parking space opposite, and where the road ceases to be enclosed.

There is a fine view from here taking in North Hessary Tor in the west (with its BBC television mast) to Hay Tor in the east, and even Fernworthy Forest can be seen peeping over a ridge away to the north.

Now follow the wall heading south towards Mel Tor. Bel Tor, left, is imprisoned among enclosures, and Venford reservoir twinkles (if the sun is shining!) 1½ miles away across the Dart valley. Jink with the track between the walls. This is the beginning of Dr Blackall's Drive, which that gentleman laid out over a hundred years ago so that he could view the scenery from the comfort of his carriage.

When the track debouches on to the open moor, bear slightly right and climb to Mel Tor to get a better appreciation of the view. Across the valley is the long rib of Bench Tor, and beneath your feet on the summit are some well-shaped rock basins (natural). Until the 1950s, after a wartime break, it was the custom on Midsummer Day to roll wagon wheels down the hillside in the hope that they would reach the river. Iron hoops may still be found at the foot of the slope.

49

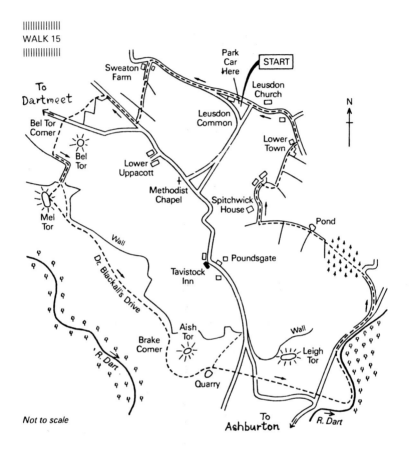

Now return to the drive and follow it along. At Brake Corner the underlying granite is left behind and the blue elvan comes to the surface. The hill farmer has cause to be grateful for the presence of elvan as ruminant animals grazing upon its slopes don't suffer from 'moorsick' as animals do in granite country. This illness is caused by a cobalt deficiency.

As the drive bears round left below Aish Tor, a tor comes into view, ahead and below — Leigh Tor. Then a tucked-away quarry is passed below the drive to the right. From here make directly for the river which is visible looping round a grassy strath ½ mile away. You will cross three roads before you reach the river.

When you arrive at the Dart follow it downstream. Note how in places the Dartmoor National Park Authority has restored the left bank where it was suffering from human erosion. This was a pioneer effort, with the gang experimenting as they proceeded, but the work seems to be

50

holding up. Where the river meets the road, get on the road and follow it for 350yd to a fork where you should turn up left (signposted 'Lowertown').

Here the walker is following the line of the Two Moors Way, a pedestrian route from Ivybridge (south Dartmoor) to Lynmouth (the Exmoor coast), officially opened in 1976. The distance is about 103 miles (165km).

At a sharp bend to the right and beside some cottages, continue straight up a track between conifer plantations. It leaves the wood, follows the bottom of three fields and meets a private road near Spitchwick House. Turn right here and follow the road (it is a public right of way) to a signposted gate (right) into a field. Now head for the second gate on the left (it is in fact the third) and follow the hedge to Lowertown. At Lowertown turn left and follow the minor road back to Leusdon Common up a fairly steep hill, and passing Leusdon Lodge Guest House which may be open to provide a welcome tea.

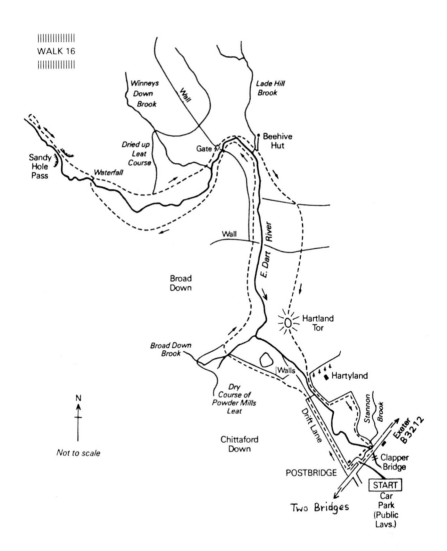

||||||||||||||
WALK 16
||||||||||||||

Winneys Down Brook

Wall

Lade Hill Brook

Beehive Hut

Sandy Hole Pass

Dried up Leat Course

Gate

Waterfall

E. Dart River

Wall

Broad Down

Hartland Tor

Broad Down Brook

Walls

Hartyland

N

Dry Course of Powder Mills Leat

Stannon Brook

Exeter B3212

Not to scale

Chittaford Down

Drift Lane

Clapper Bridge

POSTBRIDGE

START
Car Park (Public Lavs.)

Two Bridges

UP THE EAST DART RIVER FROM POSTBRIDGE

WALK 16

★

6 or 7 miles (9.5 or 11km)

Dartmoor Outdoor Leisure Map (Ordnance Survey)

This route is over open moor. It should not be attempted in bad weather unless you are accomplished in map and compass work.

Postbridge is on the B3212, and just about in the middle of the Dartmoor National Park. There is a large car park, public lavatories, a petrol station, a shop and post office, and a pub. A Dartmoor National Park information centre is open between Easter and October, and may be open at weekends in the winter.

Whether you approach Postbridge from the east or west, but especially from the east, it has the appearance of an oasis in the wilderness. There are plenty of walk possibilities from here, and that given below is one of many.

Postbridge developed in the late 18th and early 19th centuries, but never came to much. The road south to Bellever was only opened in the 1930s when the Forestry Commission started to plant the slopes of Lakehead Hill and Bellever Tor. The clapper bridge will be noticed towards the end of the walk. (Grid reference: 647 788.)

Leave the car park by the wall gap in the top corner, and turn right along Drift Lane. This is the broad path between the Archerton enclosures (left) and the East Dart river, and was the route by which cattle were driven to and from the open moor. A drift on Dartmoor means a round-up of animals.

Follow Drift Lane to its northern end where a gate gives access to a newtake, an area of enclosed moor. Keep on the gently rising track with the wall on your right, but after 100yd leave the track and stick with the wall as the track deviates left. Trace the wall to the Broad Down Brook and cross it where two branches of this stream come together at a spot where there is a broken wall. Now climb steeply to a stile up and to your right.

Having crossed the stile you will find you are on a bank with what appears to be a ditch to your left. The ditch is the dried-up course of the Powder Mills leat which drew water from the East Dart and ran it along the contours on a steadily falling course to the place between Postbridge and Two Bridges where gunpowder was once made. The water operated waterwheels for the various manufacturing processes.

If it seems strange to have had such an industry on the moor, it must be pointed out that water power was cheap, stone for building was ready to hand, space for safety was plentiful, and even labour was easy to come by at that time. Like so many Dartmoor projects it had a short life. The ruins of the mills and chimneys can be seen north of the B3212, but are invisible from here as Chittaford Down intervenes. The cottages are still occupied.

Follow the leat bank for nearly 1 mile (this is a permitted route) to where the leat was taken off the East Dart, and continue up the right bank, crossing a stile, picking your way along sheep tracks and making the best route across what becomes a steep slope, where the river runs rapidly down a gorge-like valley. Here it is sensible to stay up fairly high.

At the top of the gorge the river changes direction, so we follow it round, and 200yd from the bend reach a waterfall. The river can be crossed here, except after heavy rain when it must not be attempted. In this case the outward route back should be used, or, if time is short, a direct route over Broad Down could be taken.

From the waterfall it is possible to extend the walk for 1 mile by tracing the left bank for ½ mile to the top end of Sandy Hole Pass. This feature is a narrow defile through which the river runs after leaving Broada Marsh which is the flat area upstream from the Pass. Sandy Hole Pass can be seen as the narrow valley ¼ mile upriver from the waterfall.

The suggestion is that the walker goes as far as the upstream end to view the wilderness scene from that point. There is no problem in route-finding so long as the river is not lost sight of. Between the waterfall and Sandy Hole Pass you will pass a ruined tinners' hut standing among the debris of tin workings. Where the river runs through Sandy Hole Pass notice how its channel has been deepened and the sides built up. This was to quicken the flow and lower the water-table in the marshy area upstream, the better to work the tin-bearing gravels there.

The return walk from the waterfall starts by following the bank of another leat on the left bank. This one was about 7 or 8 miles long and took water to the mines near the Warren House Inn to work the waterwheels. After 250yd look below right for a tree 15yd below the bank where the leat bears round to the left. At this point leave the bank and head down the hillside on a line with the forest corner in the distance, then aim for a crossing point on the small side stream ahead, the Winneys Down Brook, 50yd up from its confluence with the East Dart. There is a small ford here.

Now follow a track to the hunting gate in the newtake wall ahead, staying on the path and passing a rabbit warren. Bear right above the right-angle bend of the river and cross the next stream, the Lade Hill Brook, where convenient. A curious structure, the well-known beehive hut of unknown date, may be found in a gulley on the east side of this stream 80yd up from where it falls into the Dart.

Now climb the hill slantwise and follow the ridge parallel to the river and opposite to our outward route. One wall has to be crossed, but there is a convenient gate on the east side of the ridge which should be used.

Head for Hartland Tor ahead, then drop down and aim for the point where a conifer shelter belt belonging to Hartyland meets the river. There is a path here which gets one past the field in front of the house. On reaching the rough pasture just north of Postbridge turn left along a wall (signposted) then right along the next wall, and the road is reached by the bridge.

Cross the bridge (mind the traffic!) and have a look at the clapper bridge just downstream. These bridges are hard to date, and may not be as old as they look. This one is the best on the moor and was probably built in the 13th century. One can only marvel at their ability to withstand flood water. I have seen a photograph showing a torrent lapping the underside of the horizontal spans!

The car park is now just a stone's throw away.

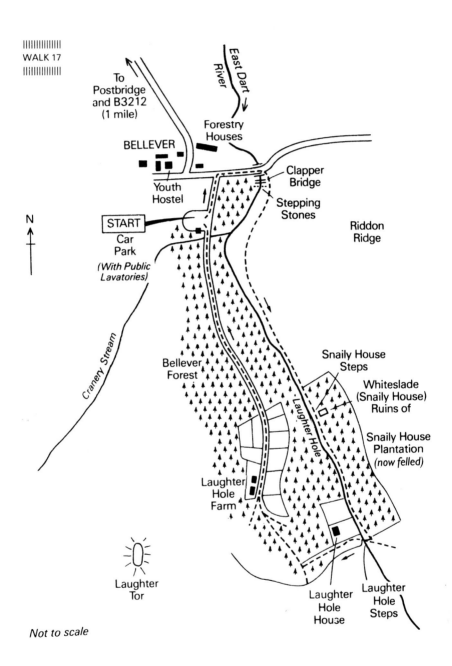

To
Postbridge
and B3212
(1 mile)

East Dart
River

Forestry
Houses

BELLEVER

Youth
Hostel

Clapper
Bridge

Stepping
Stones

N

Riddon
Ridge

START
Car
Park
(With Public
Lavatories)

Cranery Stream

Bellever
Forest

Snaily House
Steps

Whiteslade
(Snaily House)
Ruins of

Snaily House
Plantation
(now felled)

Laughter Hole

Laughter
Hole
Farm

Laughter
Tor

Laughter
Hole
House

Laughter
Hole
Steps

Not to scale

BELLEVER AND
THE EAST DART RIVER

WALK 17

★

3 miles (4.8km)

Dartmoor Outdoor Leisure Map (Ordnance Survey)

This is an easy walk with no steep climbs, but if the river is running high the stepping stones at the halfway point should not be attempted.

Bellever is a Forestry Commission hamlet with a Youth Hostel, built round an ancient farm. It is reached along a minor road 1 mile south of the B3212 at Postbridge in the middle of the moor. The tree-screened car park is between the houses and the river. There are public lavatories. (Grid reference: 656 772.)

From the car park walk back 200yd to the tarmac road and turn right towards the bridge over the East Dart. From the bridge the earlier clapper bridge can be seen just downstream with an incomplete line of stepping stones beyond.

William Crossing wrote (*Amid Devonia's Alps*, 1888, reprinted 1974) that he knew the man who admitted to having thrown off the missing central stone 'when a boy'. Apart from the feat of strength this would have been for a boy, even allowing for an understanding of rock manipulation we have largely forgotten, there is no trace of the dislodged stone. But there is the existing evidence of six mortises (grooves), three on each pier, which could have provided a secure lodgement for three wooden cross pieces which themselves supported a gangway of wooden slats. This seems a much more likely explanation for the missing span.

Cross the bridge and walk down the east (left) bank. The forest which stretches away in every direction except over Riddon Ridge to the east began to be planted between the wars. Most of the trees are different varieties of spruce. In the 1960s the Forestry Commission established the car park and a picnic site on the river bank where the Cranery Stream falls into the East Dart. As you walk along you will see that the National Park Authority has had to rebuild the river banks here as they had become eroded from people-pressure.

Stay on the river bank and pass through a broken wall into Snaily House plantation (now felled). Many acres have been clear-felled across the river, and in some places have been re-planted. About 100yd into the plantation a ruin will be seen to your left. This is Whiteslade, or Snaily House as it has come to be known.

Many years ago in that hazy era known as 'once upon a time' the local people were puzzled as to how the two elderly spinsters who lived there managed to look so well fed while keeping no animals and tending no garden. Perhaps they were stealing others' sheep, it was suggested! So a watch was kept, but no light was shed on the problem. Eventually a deputation marched up to the door, was admitted and got the answer: rows of pans containing slugs pickled in salt. Their secret out, the women pined away and died, and the house sank into ruin. This happened early in the 19th century. When the house was occupied, some way of crossing the river was required, and Snaily House stepping stones can be seen in the river opposite the ruin.

This stretch of the river is called Laughter Hole, from the tor of that name, Laughter Tor, up the hill to the west; a 'hole' on Dartmoor is a steep-sided narrow valley. At the foot of the steepest section is Laughter Hole House, built between the wars and one of the most isolated dwellings on the moor still inhabited, although there is an associated farm not far away. Laughter Hole House always seems to me as if it was designed for an Indian hill station.

At the southern end of Snaily House plantation cross to the west side using Laughter Hole stepping stones beside Win Ford. These were re-set in the late 1980s, and are now much safer to use than previously. Now follow the good path round the outside of the house garden to a gate leading into the forest of small trees. Walk 200yd up this path, turn right at a signpost and follow this tack for 1 mile back to the car park. Laughter Hole farm and its fields will be passed on the way.

DARTMEET TO COMBESTONE TOR

WALK 18

★

3 miles (4.8km)

Dartmoor Outdoor Leisure Map (Ordnance Survey)

A long but fairly gentle climb to start, and two lines of slippery stepping stones, make this a walk for well-shod fit people in summer, when there is little water flowing down. The stepping stones should not be attempted if the river is running high, and if the first line of stones is difficult to cross the second line will be impassable! (Having said this, the Dartmoor National Park Authority re-set the Laughter Hole stepping stones (Walk 17) in the late 1980s to make them easier to cross, so they may get round to doing the same to the West Dart stepping stones.)

Dartmeet is a popular beauty spot on the Ashburton to Two Bridges road. There is a large restaurant, and there are public lavatories. Walkers should note that the Dartmeet car park is privately owned, so it would be expedient not to use it for long-term parking for groups, and on busy days in the summer and on Sundays. (Grid reference: 672 733.)

From the car park, walk across the bridge, noting the storm-ruined clapper bridge just upstream. The actual meeting point of the two Dart rivers, the East and West, is just downstream from here, and many visitors never see it. The united river is sometimes called the Double Dart.

Pass through the forecourt of an old filling station and walk 20yd down a signposted path to a gate. Enter the field, turn left, and cross the West Dart by a line of stepping stones. (See the cautionary note in the first paragraph above.) From the south bank follow the path indicated by the signpost up through a pleasant mixture of trees and rocks to a gate leading into a field. Keep beside the left-hand wall, making for a gap in the wall ahead, and go through the gap still keeping the wall on your left.

Abreast of Combestone farm a signpost points the way uphill, still beside the wall, to a gate beside a wooden shed. Go through this gate, now following the farm track to the next gate where the open moor is reached. Mark this spot, as after a visit to Combestone Tor which is visible 400yd ahead we will return here. Now head for Combestone Tor (pronounced 'Cumston') striding or jumping a leat on the way. A dry leat is also crossed halfway to the tor.

At the tor, climb to the top of one of the rock piles for a good view. To the south the high land of southern Dartmoor swells up, broken by the valley of the O Brook, the shortest placename in England. Across the

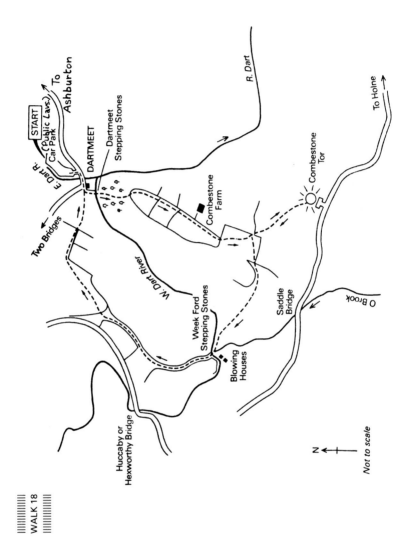

WALK 18

Not to scale

N ←

valley to the north, pick out the ruined prehistoric parallel field-banks on the facing hillside. These are locally called reaves, and a well-illustrated book called *The Dartmoor Reaves* by Andrew Fleming (Batsford, 1988) describes these fascinating land divisions in an attractive way. At your feet, as you stand on the tor, are naturally-eroded basins or hollows, a testament to the severity of the weather over millions of years.

Now return to the gate on the farm track, pass through it, and bear left as indicated by the sign reading 'Bridlepath to Week Ford stepping stones'. At the time of writing, this section as far as the river is not well defined, but so long as you realise that Week Ford is just upstream from where the O Brook enters the West Dart you can make for the point where the two valleys converge. A footbridge passes over the O Brook, and the stepping stones are 100yd up the West Dart from here, but before attempting to cross, measure the risks carefully. There are no rights of way up or down river, so a return to the outward route will have to be made if you decide not to risk an immersion.

Before crossing, it is worth looking at the nearby ruins of two quite well-preserved blowing (or smelting) mills. They are tucked away under a steep bank among some trees on the south side, and were used in medieval times to extract tin from locally dug ore. Mortar and mould stones lie around, and waterwheels supplied the power for the various processes.

Assuming the stepping stones have been negotiated, from the north side of the river walk up the lane which gradually bears round to the right. Pass through a gate, go past a large shed and silage pit, and into a field through a waymarked gate. Now make for the top right-hand corner of this field. A signpost stands on the skyline indicating the way, but it is used as a rubbing post and can be pushed over. Exit from the field through a gate in a dip with converging cattle tracks leading to it, and walk down the lane for 200yd to a stile admitting one to a narrower lane. 50yd further on a gate to the left allows you to enter the top corner of the field you passed through at the beginning of the walk.

Make for the far bottom corner and the car park is reached in a few minutes by re-crossing the river bridge.

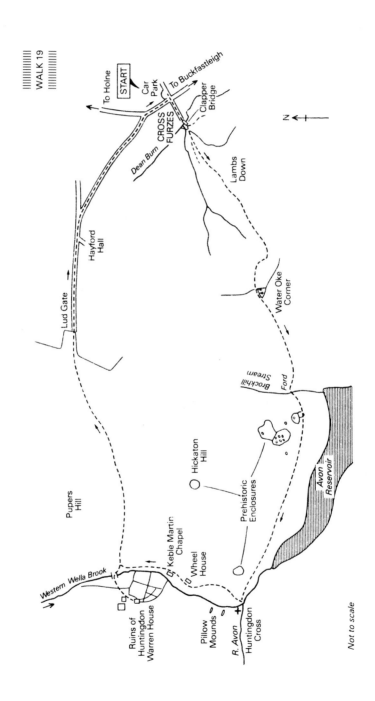

To Holne

START

Car
Park

To Buckfastleigh

Clapper
Bridge

CROSS
FURZES

Dean Burn

Lambs
Down

N

Hayford
Hall

Water Oke
Corner

Lud Gate

Brockhill
Stream

Ford

Pupers
Hill

Hickaton
Hill

Avon
Reservoir

Prehistoric
Enclosures

Keble Martin
Chapel

Wheel
House

Western Wella Brook

Ruins of
Huntingdon
Warren House

Pillow
Mounds

R. Avon

Huntingdon
Cross

Not to scale

THE ABBOTS' WAY AND HUNTINGDON WARREN

WALK 19

★

6 miles (9.5km)

Dartmoor Outdoor Leisure Map (Ordnance Survey)

An open moor walk, apart from a mile at the beginning and end, so this should not be attempted in mist unless you are accomplished with map and compass. The enjoyment of the walk will be greatly enhanced if you take with you a copy of the Dartmoor National Park booklet *The Archaeology of Dartmoor*. The aerial photograph on page 13 shows in great detail a part of the moor covered in this walk.

The walk begins at Cross Furzes, a signposted crossroads 2½ miles up a long lane from Buckfastleigh. From Buckfastleigh turn up Wallaford Road. Park you car in the layby near the crossroads. (Grid reference: 699 668.)

Walk down the rough track from the crossroads (signposted as a right of way) to the two-span clapper bridge over the Dean Burn. This is one of the best of these bridges on the moor because of its situation and completeness, and the fact that various initials and dates are inscribed thereon. The date 1737 is easily deciphered.

Pass through the gate beyond the bridge and take the right fork. The path goes up Lambs Down following a line of marker posts. Ignore a well-worn track which pursues a course lower down the hillside. Your immediate destination is Water Oke Corner, a scattering of scrappy, storm-shattered trees in a triangular enclosure where the fields meet the moor (replanted in the 1980s), but the path bends round a small stream to save a steep climb.

This is the line of the so-called Abbots' Way. Some Dartmoor writers have suggested it was a cross-Dartmoor route between Buckfast Abbey on the eastern border of the moor, and the abbeys of Buckland and Tavistock on the west. But the name is first found as late as 1790, so the proposition may be without foundation. The route is somewhat incomplete; here it certainly exists, but once on the moor it is less so.

Go through the gate on to the open moor, noting as you do so how the wall to your right is faced as a wall to the moor, but has a gently sloping bank on the field side. This is known as a cornditch. In medieval times the king's deer sometimes roamed onto enclosed land and, though meant to deter them, these banked walls would allow the deer to escape should they get in.

63

The view is good from here. Widecombe church tower can be seen in the cleavage of the East Webburn valley, and Teignmouth stands at the outfall of the estuary, with the sea beyond. Now walk uphill parallel with the wall on your left, keeping straight on when the corner is passed. The direction is slightly south of west, and 200yd after the wall is left behind, the summit cairn of Eastern Whittabarrow will be seen $1^1/2$ miles away if the day is clear, looking rather like a nuclear submarine stranded ark-like on the Ararat which is Brent Moor! Aim for the cairn, and when going down the other side of this easily graded hill the Avon reservoir comes into view, and the point to make for now is the ford in the side-valley ahead.

Cross this stream — the Brockhill Stream — at Brockhill Ford, and carry on along the obvious track which is once again the (presumed) Abbots' Way. About 300yd beyond the ford a fine collection of Bronze Age huts and enclosures can be seen, right, near the track, and are worth deviating slightly to examine.

The reservoir was built between 1954 and 1957 to supply south Devon, and the water surface, when full, is 50 acres in extent.

The way is clear for $^3/4$ mile beyond the prehistoric remains, where a side-stream comes in from the north. This is the Western Wella Brook. Beyond the stream is Huntingdon Cross, a simple monument of unknown age. These isolated crosses don't mark graves, but were probably erected in an age of piety to mark a route.

There is no need to cross the Western Wella Brook, but make your way up the east (left) bank of the brook, picking your way between the wet patches of ground. If you have got with you the booklet mentioned at the beginning of this walk you are now progressing from left to right across the middle of the aerial photograph on page 13. You thread your way among the waste tips of the medieval tin-streamers. On the hillside across the brook are many pillow mounds aligned downslope. These were made by the warrener at Huntingdon Warren (upstream) as artificial breeding sites for the rabbits which were bred here for flesh and fur in the 19th century.

The ruined stone walls $^1/2$ mile up the brook shielded a 19th century waterwheel from the wind. The wheel was used to pump a mine some distance away, and the water came from the brook. The leat embankment is 80yd to the north. In a gulley 10yd west of the embankment is a small open-to-the-sky chapel with an upright stone at the top end bearing an incised cross. This little place of worship was built by the Martin brothers in 1909 when they were camped near Huntingdon Cross. Many years later, one of them, Keble Martin, became the best-selling author/illustrator of *The Concise British Flora*.

Across the stream are the ruins of Huntingdon Warren house, and upstream, the approach track crosses the brook by a primitive bridge of five lengths of stone laid side by side.

Now take the track going east over the shoulder of Pupers Hill, and down to Lud Gate. Another mile brings the walker back to his car at Cross Furzes

THE AVON VALLEY AND SHIPLEY BRIDGE

WALK 20

★

5 or 8 miles (8 or 12km)

Dartmoor Outdoor Leisure Map (Ordnance Survey)

This is a fairly gentle walk, part path, part quiet road. Park your car at the Dartmoor end of the car park on the site of South Brent station and railway goods yard. The station closed in 1964. South Brent is nearly at the southernmost tip of the National Park, and is just off the A38 dual carriageway.

Before setting off on the walk as described, have a look around the small town. The church is especially interesting, being different from most Dartmoor churches. The massive Norman tower was once the central tower of a cruciform building, but the western part was demolished, probably in the 14th century. Look out for the conspicuous market toll house in the main street, still exhibiting its 1889 scale of tolls. There are a couple of interesting old pubs, and the Anchor Hotel was a staging house for the London coaches. (Grid reference: 697 603.)

From the car park turn left on to the railway bridge approach, then at once right down a signposted path beside a house called 'Riverside'. The path goes beneath the railway then follows the river Avon to Lydia Bridge. Look out for many birds along here, particularly the robin, wren, tree creeper and dipper. The latter, a black bird with a white breast, bobs about on the stones in the river, and sometimes walks beneath its surface. The path is supposed to be haunted by a monk in a red habit.

Lydia Bridge is approached by time-smoothed steps. On the bridge, turn left and continue 150yd along. Round the first corner a signposted stile is seen right. This admits the walker to a narrow path between walls. It bears left and crosses a stone slab stile into a field. From here to the next road follow the yellow waymarks, but the route is as described. Make for the next stile slightly uphill and ⅔ of the way along the top hedge. Continue to the next slab stile visible ahead. Now climb slightly uphill, making for a stile in the next hedge where the woodland peters out. From here make for the roof of a cottage 200yd away where a stile gives access to the road. Turn right and follow this road to Shipley Bridge, taking the right fork on the way. The large sprawl of buildings you will pass is the former Didworthy Hospital. At Shipley Bridge there is a pleasant open space, and it is from here that the walk can be extended up-river along a tarmac road beside the river. However, you

65

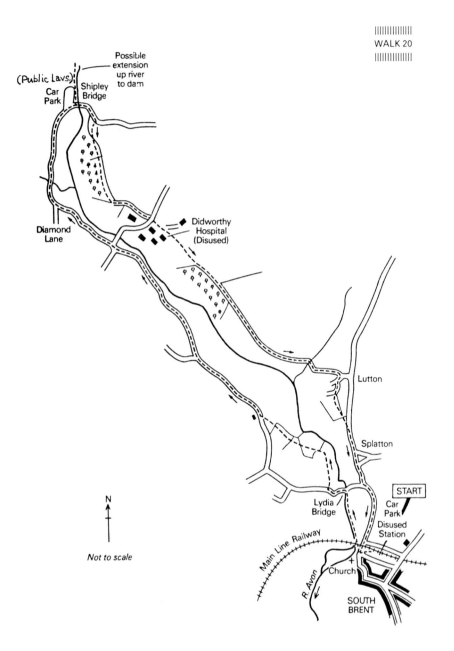

Possible
extension
up river
to dam

(Public Lavs.)
Car
Park

Shipley
Bridge

Diamond
Lane

Didworthy
Hospital
(Disused)

Lutton

Splatton

START

Car
Park

N

Disused
Station

Lydia
Bridge

Not to scale

Main Line Railway

Church

R. Avon

SOUTH
BRENT

should not be troubled by traffic as it is a South West Water road. For much of the way it is a designated bridleway.

The road leads directly to the dam of the Avon reservoir (built 1954–7) and passes through fine river-valley scenery on the way. So long as you stay on the road no further directions need be given. The extra distance is 5 miles there and back, but of course you can shorten the walk at any stage by turning back.

There are several features to look out for. The Hunters' Stone, 300yd up-river from the bridge, is a large stone beside the road, bearing the incised names of celebrated huntsmen of the past. Then, as one passes through a narrow part of the valley somewhat overgrown with rhododendrons, a small memorial to a little girl who was drowned in the river in 1863 will be seen on a rock to your left. Immediately past this are the ruins of Brent Moor House, originally a private house, latterly a Youth Hostel, and finally demolished in 1968 after being empty for some time.

The massive stone walls at Shipley Bridge were built in connection with the china clay working at Redlake, miles away in the middle of southern Dartmoor. The clay was brought here on a wooden-railed tramway for processing.

Now cross the bridge to the east side and walk 200yd to the cattle grid, and enter a signposted and waymarked path. Initially it climbs, then levels out and follows the top edge of woodland. Just before the former hospital it drops steeply down a rough lane to meet a road in the midst of the complex, and there is a signpost here.

Carry straight on, climbing through an impressive grove of stately beeches. The way is clear from here, and follows a mixture of field edges and ancient lanes with fine views across the valley. Just before Lutton is reached the lane drops steeply to a ford with a single-span clapper bridge beside it, then climbs to Lutton Green. At the letterbox turn right, bear left before a large house and enter a gate facing you. By keeping the hedge to your left you will now be led via a couple of stiles to the Brent road. Turn right and South Brent is reached in ¾ mile.

HARFORD AND THE ERME VALLEY

WALK 21

★

4½ miles (7km)

Dartmoor Outdoor Leisure Map (Ordnance Survey)

This is a gentle walk, but there is a likelihood of mud after rain. Park your car on the approach to the disused station at Ivybridge, which is the town at the southern extremity of the National Park. Drive up the west side of the Erme from the town, under the railway viaduct, and turn sharp left just beyond. (Grid reference: 636 569.) A new station, one mile to the east, was built for Ivybridge a few years ago.

From the old station approach, walk towards the river Erme, and notice the old piers (uprights) of the bridge which were part of Brunel's original viaduct and pre-dated the present structure. The old piers bore a timber superstructure.

Take the signposted road heading south uphill. This is the approach road to Pithill farm, and a public right of way. (There is a footpath lower down the slope near the Erme, but the route described here ignores this route which was opened in the 1980s.)

At Pithill the route bears left and where the lane turns left by a large shed the walker should enter the right-hand gate and keep the hedge on your left. There are now superb views ahead of southern Dartmoor with the Erme valley in the middle distance.

When the path reaches the isolated farm of Wilkeys Moor, use the ladder stiles provided to circumvent the farmyard. The path then continues beyond the farm along an ancient lane, which bears left and ends at a field gate. Follow the bottom hedge, then cross a field to a hunting gate and enter scrubland. The path is now clear to the next hunting gate where a wood is entered. Take the left path 10yd inside the gate, the right path is private. Leave the wood and enter a field, turning right and making for a gate in the north corner. Now go straight across the field to a wall corner from where a straight lane leading to the road at Hall farm is used.

At the road turn right and follow it to the tiny village of Harford. The church is worth visiting. It has a good ceiling and a brass in the chancel. Notice also a curious round-headed memorial to John Prideaux and his wife, made of painted copper.

Leave the rook-clattering churchyard by the lychgate, and 20yd up the lane enter Butterbrook drive. About 100yd along here enter a gate left, and follow the field edge down to a clapper bridge with a hunting gate. Now climb the rocky field on a well-marked path to an iron kissing gate. Pass through here and head for the top of the field when the next iron

68

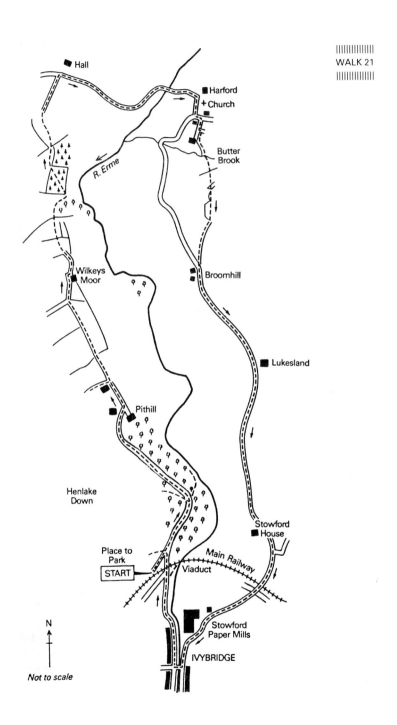

Hall

Harford
+ Church

Butter
Brook

R. Erme

Wilkeys
Moor

Broomhill

Lukesland

Pithill

Henlake
Down

Stowford
House

Place to
Park

START

Main Railway

Viaduct

Stowford
Paper Mills

IVYBRIDGE

N

Not to scale

gate is visible ahead. Enter this gate and head for a wooden gate on the opposite side of the field. Then follow the left-hand hedge to a large stone slab stile which gives access to a grassy corner and the road 15yd beyond.

The road is now followed back to Ivybridge. The fine stone house, Lukesland, which cannot easily be seen from the road, was used as Baskerville Hall by a film crew producing *The Hound of the Baskervilles* some years ago.

Just beyond the railway bridge a stone will be seen at the roadside inscribed 'Two Moors Way 29 May 1976'. This commemorates the opening of this long-distance footpath from Ivybridge, across Dartmoor, Mid-Devon and Exmoor, to Lynmouth on the North Devon coast. A guidebook describes its route.

As the route drops steeply down into Ivybridge, the 1862 Stowford Paper Mills of Wiggins Teape are passed, and you cross the Erme by the original Ivy Bridge, still with some ivy growing upon it. Turn right, and a short walk brings you back to the car.

TROWLESWORTHY AND THE PLYM VALLEY

WALK 22

★

2 miles (3km)

Dartmoor Outdoor Leisure Map (Ordnance Survey)

This is a gentle walk suitable for young and old, but take care in bad weather. The start of the walk is 700yd east of Cadover Bridge, where the river Plym leaves the open moor, and standing on the minor road which runs between Ivybridge and Yelverton. Park your car where a gravel track leaves the road and heads for Trowlesworthy farm.

The eye-catching features hereabouts are the china clay workings. The kaolinization of granite, its chemical decomposition, produces this white substance which is in demand for crockery and as an inert filler for cosmetics, paper, rubber, plastics and paint. Some of the waste is used to make building blocks and bricks, but the rest is piled up beside the pits. The workings began in the 1830s. (Grid reference: 564 644.)

Walk along the rough track away from the road, and cross the bridge over the Blacka Brook. Here you enter National Trust property which extends up the Plym valley as far as Plym Head.

As the track rises, notice the humps and bumps across the river. These are the tailings of old stream tin workings. The gravels and stones of the valley bottom were worked over for tin-bearing rocks. The area is known as Brisworthy Burrows.

After a small cutting, where the track bears right, continue straight ahead towards a wall corner. Beside the corner, to the left of the path, is a rabbit bury, an artificially-prepared rabbit burrow. Trowlesworthy was one of several warrens in the Plym valley, providing meat throughout the year before the days of refrigeration, with the skins as a by-product. Trowlesworthy was the last warren to carry on this trade on Dartmoor, having begun about 1300. It became legally impossible to breed wild rabbits in the 1950s when the opportunity was taken of the myxomatosis epidemic to attempt to eradicate the rabbit altogether.

Contour along, and at the far end of an enclosure to the left, cross an old wall and bear up right passing ancient enclosures. Make for Shadyback Tor, 150yd ahead. This is a fairly small rockpile, unnamed on the Ordnance Survey maps.

Look across the Plym from here. Legis Tor is opposite, and the Legis Lake (perversely a lake is a small stream on Dartmoor!) flows into the Plym below where we are standing. Its course has been much turned

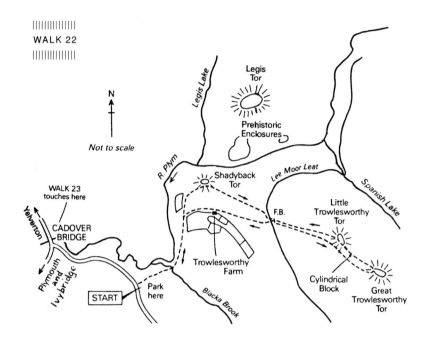

over by the medieval tin streamers. Between Legis Tor and the river are the tell-tale ruined walls of Bronze Age enclosures.

Now turn away and head uphill on a line with Little Trowlesworthy Tor. At the Lee Moor leat, which provides water for the Plym for the clay works, cross the leat by one of several bridges.

Head straight for the nearest rocks of the tor, 900yd ahead, looking out for some fine Bronze Age ruined huts on the slope. At the tor you will see a small quarry on its north side, and much squared and cut stone lying about. The stone of Trowlesworthy, being red granite, was in demand for ornamental purposes. Between Little Trowlesworthy Tor and Great Trowlesworthy Tor, 400yd beyond, is a conspicuous stunted stone cylinder which was cut in 1823 with the intention of using it as a flagpole base in connection with Devonport's independence celebrations, but for some reason it was never finished.

To return, make for the right side of Trowlesworthy farm. There is a rabbit bury near the wall as you approach the house and another beyond the last building. You will also notice the ruins of huts and ancient enclosures. Surely it is a miracle they have survived so long and have not been plundered for subsequent building purposes? The track is to your left now, and will take you back to the starting point of the walk.

THE DEWERSTONE AND THE MIDDLE REACH OF THE RIVER PLYM

WALK 23

★

4 miles (6.5km)

Dartmoor Outdoor Leisure Map (Ordnance Survey)

There is a not-too-steep climb at the start of this varied walk; it is then fairly level. Walk 22 could be grafted on to the route at the halfway point to increase its length by 2 miles.

Leave your car in the car park at Shaugh Bridge, which is at the meeting of the rivers Meavy and Plym, 2 miles east of the main A386 where it crosses Roborough Down just north of Plymouth. (Grid reference: 533 636.)

To get your bearings, first stand on Shaugh Bridge itself. This is sited just downstream from the confluence of the rivers Meavy (left) and Plym (right). The present bridge dates from the 1820s and replaced a bridge severely damaged by a flood in January 1823. On that occasion the moor had been covered with snow, but a sudden thaw, combined with heavy rain, caused the rivers to rise with catastrophic effect.

Now cross the footbridge to the National Trust property between the two rivers, and take the wide path rising on the river Plym side of the promontory. The path is rough and rocky and climbs steadily and straight to a sharp bend to the left. Here it levels out and passes a small quarry, then bends to the right, passing between a 15ft rock pinnacle and a large block of rock. In fact the track was cut through the granite here.

It is obvious from the carefully graded track that we are now on the line of a railway system constructed to remove stone from the various quarries on the hillside. The path descends slightly, then a straight uphill section is seen ahead, right. Go up here and notice the stone sleepers still in situ. The rails have gone.

This was an inclined plane. Two parallel tracks operated simultaneously; the full trucks descending pulled the empty trucks up, rather like a cliff railway. At the top are the remains of the cable drum house, with the spindle still visible. Just below the top, notice how generations of badgers have excavated heaps of earth across the inclined plane.

Now take a path going gently upwards to the right, passing small quarries with tips opposite and rejected squared stones scattered about. Where the railway clearly ended, continue uphill, and the summit rocks are reached just beyond the tree line. This is the top of the Dewerstone,

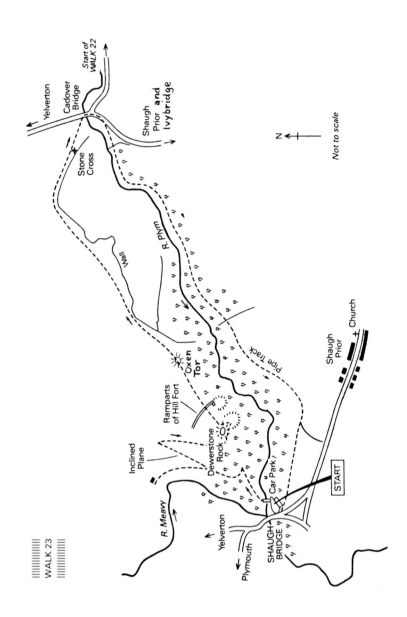

WALK 23

Yelverton
Cadover Bridge
Start of WALK 22
Shaugh Prior and Ivybridge

Stone Cross

Wall

R. Plym

Oxen Tor

Ramparts of Hill Fort

Pipe Track

Inclined Plane

Dewerstone Rock

Car Park

Shaugh Prior

Church

START

SHAUGH BRIDGE

R. Meavy

Yelverton

Plymouth

N

Not to scale

and various inscriptions can be seen cut in the rocks, notably the one to N. T. Carrington, who published a lengthy poem about Dartmoor in 1826. At one time it was suggested that a memorial might be raised to him up here, to be executed by the architect John Wightwick, but the scheme came to nothing. Instead one finds the words 'Carrington — Obiit Septembris MDCCCXXX' incised in the rock. Carrington is buried at Combe Hay near Bath.

Now take in the view. Plymouth Breakwater is plainly seen, and near at hand is Bickleigh Camp (Royal Marines). Our return route is visible contouring the hillside to the south.

Before setting off across the open moor, go down about 80yd along a green path to get a top view of the main rock-climbing faces which are on the Plym side of this great thrusting spur. They will be seen again from across the valley. The Dewerstone gives the best rock climbing on Dartmoor. In 1960 a climber found a late Bronze Age (1000 BC) drinking cup in a rock crevice here. It is now in Plymouth Museum.

Return to the summit and head north-east, making for the prominent rocks — not named on any Ordnance Survey map, but known as Oxen Tor — in line with the top edge of the woods beyond. As you leave the Dewerstone spur you will pass through the ruins of two dry-stone walls. These were defensive ramparts thrown up by Iron Age people when the summit was used as a promontory fort. In the same way many coastal headlands were developed as refuges in times of inter-tribal warfare.

After passing Oxen Tor the route to follow is along the outside of the enclosure walls, and after 1 mile this will bring you down to Cadover Bridge past a stone cross standing in a socket stone which is itself sited within a circular earthwork. The modern shaft is of red granite, presumably from Trowlesworthy Tor (see Walk 22). This cross was discovered by troops exercising here in 1873 and set up by them. From here the china clay works are much in evidence — see Walk 22 for details.

Cross the road bridge, turn right and follow the river bank. On reaching the fence, climb the signposted stile which is about 20yd from the river. The path follows a broken pipeline and is waymarked with yellow blobs where route-finding might be difficult. The pipe carried china clay in suspension to the Shaugh Bridge drying works and as a result this is called the Pipe Track.

The further you walk along this path, the more the crags of the Dewerstone become visible opposite, perhaps with climbers clinging to them. When the path meets a dirt road this is used for a short distance, but should be left at a stile and the signposted and waymarked path followed steeply downhill through the woods after leaving a field. On reaching the road, turn sharp right along a level track then descend a flight of steep stone steps safeguarded by a double handrail. This brings you back to the car park by the ruins of the china clay 'drys'.

BURRATOR RESERVOIR

WALK 24

★

4 miles (6.5km)

Dartmoor Outdoor Leisure Map (Ordnance Survey)

This is a simple level walk which is suitable for parents with a pushchair as it follows the public tarmac road round the reservoir. Two short diversions can be added, and these are included in the distance given above. It is not very enjoyable on a day when a lot of cars are on the move.

Burrator reservoir is reached by turning off the B3212 at Dousland, 1½ miles from Yelverton. Park near the dam.

The reservoir was formed in 1898 to solve the water storage problems of the expanding city of Plymouth. The dam was heightened in 1928 to increase the capacity, and while this was being done traffic reached Sheepstor by a suspension bridge strung across the arm of the reservoir beside the dam. (Grid reference: 551 681.)

Leave the area of the dam and walk along the western side of the reservoir, keeping right at the fork just beyond Burrator Lodge. The pre-reservoir approach to Sheepstor was down a lane opposite the north gate of the Lodge.

From the tail of the reservoir there is a fine view up to Leather Tor, which has been likened to the Matterhorn as seen from Zermatt! Certainly it is one of the most dramatic of Dartmoor's 200 or so tors — from this angle.

At the end of the reservoir continue around, ignoring tracks off to the left, and follow the road along the east side. About ⅔ mile along here pay a visit to the very interesting Longstone peninsula which juts out into the reservoir.

Climb the stile beside the iron gate and look at the forlorn fenced ruins of Longstone Manor. Nearby are a variety of stone remains: five stone troughs, a crusher and edge-runner. At the water's edge beyond the ruin is another trough. About 50yd from the ruin, but invisible from it because of the trees, is a windstrew or winnowing platform. Here the threshing was done, allowing the breezes to carry off the chaff. Now walk round the promontory, taking care not to disturb any anglers or the fish. The shoreline path will bring you back to the starting point as the peninsula is almost an island.

Back on the road resume your circumnavigation of the reservoir. Where the road veers away from the reservoir, a short cut can be made across the Sheepstor earth-filled dam, but this will mean missing the

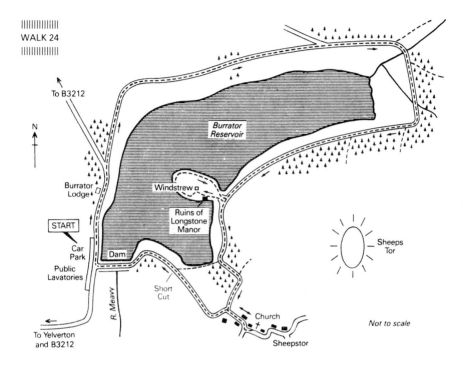

To B3212

N

Burrator Reservoir

Burrator Lodge

Windstrew □

START

Ruins of Longstone Manor

Car Park

Public Lavatories

Dam

Short Cut

Sheeps Tor

Not to scale

R. Meavy

Church

To Yelverton and B3212

Sheepstor

diversion to the village itself, so if a visit to Sheepstor is desired carry on along the road to the next T-junction and turn left to view the tiny village which takes its name from the tor which looms up behind.

Seek out the elaborate tombs of the Brooke family at the top of the churchyard. These were the famous white rajahs of Sarawak, uncle and nephew, who ruled that far eastern country during the last century. Sir John Brooke died at Burrator House, near the dam, in 1868. Later it was occupied by C. E. Brittan, probably the most accomplished Dartmoor painter, who is also buried in the churchyard.

Bull-baiting was formerly carried out in the vicarage field near the church. A bull was secured to a well-anchored rock and then baited, or tormented, by dogs. At these barbarous festivities the women wore special aprons in which they caught the bulldog when it was thrown. It was the custom to bury on the spot the dogs which were killed.

Now retrace your steps to the T-junction, and take the road heading down past the Old School House. The dam and car park are reached in about ⅓ mile.

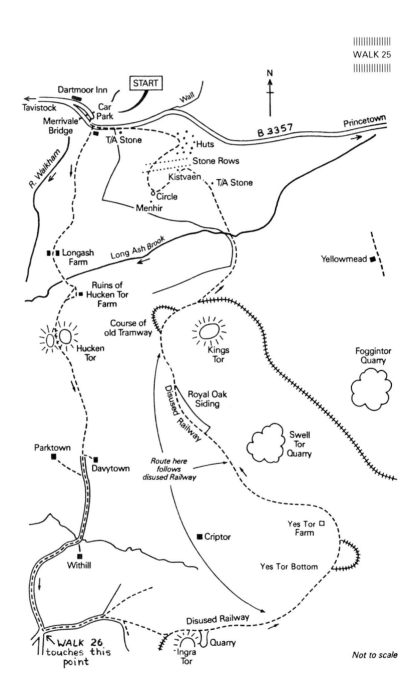

N

Dartmoor Inn

START

Wall

Tavistock

Car Park

Merrivale Bridge

T/A Stone

B 3357

Princetown

R. Walkham

Huts

Stone Rows

Kistvaen

T/A Stone

Circle

Menhir

Longash Farm

Long Ash Brook

Yellowmead

Ruins of Hucken Tor Farm

Course of old Tramway

Hucken Tor

Kings Tor

Foggintor Quarry

Disused Railway

Royal Oak Siding

Swell Tor Quarry

Parktown

Davytown

Route here follows disused Railway

Yes Tor Farm

Criptor

Withill

Yes Tor Bottom

Disused Railway

WALK 26 touches this point

Ingra Tor

Quarry

Not to scale

THE WALKHAM VALLEY AND THE MERRIVALE ANTIQUITIES

WALK 25

★

6 miles (9.5km)

Dartmoor Outdoor Leisure Map (Ordnance Survey)

This is a varied walk on tracks and open moor, with little climbing. There is trackless moor at the end, so take care in mist.

Park your car by the old bridge over the river Walkham, near the Dartmoor Inn at Merrivale, on the B3357 between Tavistock and Two Bridges. (Grid reference: 550 751.)

Climb up the embankment to the 'new' road, cross it, and enter the signposted farm track beside Hillside Cottages. The heaps of worked stone inside the gate were dumped here when the Napoleonic War warders' quarters in Princetown were demolished in the 1960s.

A quarry is passed, then Long Ash farm. Across the valley is Vixen Tor, a magnificent pile, perhaps seen at its best from here. It can be climbed, but is quite a scramble. Do not attempt it from here, as the permitted approach is from the far side.

Carry on along the track and cross the Long Ash Brook (sometimes called the Pila Brook). Where the track leaves the woods head uphill for 50yd or so, and you will find the low ruined walls of Hucken Tor farm. The most distinctive features are the twelve upright stones of the rickyard. They served to keep the ricks off the ground and away from rats and damp, and allowed air to circulate. Also here are the remains of the farmhouse and outbuildings.

Return now to the track and follow it along to Hucken Tor, a charming feature, much grown around with trees and covered with moss. A gate is actually built between the rocks of the tor, and passing through a fine view opens up ahead.

The track is now straightforward and generally downhill for well over 1 mile and turns into a tarred road. Three farms are passed: Parktown (right) and Davytown and Withill (left). At the first crossroads turn up left, signposted to Criptor (the north-east corner of Walk 26 touches this point), and after crossing a cattle grid take a track heading off right towards Ingra Tor. Where this track bears right, keep straight on, and the line of the disused Princetown branch railway is reached just before the tor.

Turn left along the track, east, and where it passes the mouth of a quarry digress briefly to look inside. It is quite deep. This railway began

79

life as a horse-drawn tramway in the 1820s, was later converted to a conventional railway, and closed in 1956. For the last twenty years of its life there was a stopping place here called Ingra Tor Halt which exhibited a sign reading:

Great Western Railway Company
NOTICE
In the interests of game preservation and
for their own protection against snakes,
dogs should be kept on a lead.
By order

The line continues round the small valley called Yes Tor Bottom. Notice how the original tramway followed a longer route. Being a tramway it could use curves of a tighter radius. Other examples of this route variation will be seen further on. The ruins of Yes Tor farm on the lower side of the track are passed, and it is worth noting that to cope with the gradient the railway had to travel 2½ miles before doubling back to a point just 400yd uphill from here.

The line straightens out somewhat, and the remains of the Royal Oak Siding, which led to Swell Tor quarry, are seen on the right. Then the line starts its compass-boxing bend and the course of the old tramway is very noticeable.

Stay on the track until the yellow front of Yellowmead farm comes into view on the lower slopes of North Hessary Tor. Now cut down left and head north-east to a wall corner. Follow the wall to a stream, the headwaters of the Long Ash Brook crossed earlier. At the stream, head for a tall stone breaking the skyline ahead. (Ignore a larger stone away to your left; this is a prehistoric menhir.)

When you have reached the stone you are heading for, notice that it bears two letters, a T and an A. These stand for Tavistock and Ashburton and are clues to the purpose of the stone. It was one of a number erected as guidestones for travellers across this stretch of moor, and probably dates from about 1700.

Now aim for Merrivale quarry on the slopes of Staple Tor. Your course will take you to the Bronze Age remains usually known as the Merrivale antiquities, 200yd from the T/A stone.

Two stone rows (see Introduction for a general account of Dartmoor antiquities) run parallel to each other and should be visited first. Walk along the southernmost row. A few yards to your left you will see the despoiled capstone of a kistvaen. The chest itself is undamaged, but someone cut a gatepost or mantlepiece out of the lid. Back at the row a burial site marks the halfway point, and just beyond, another burial mound away from the row seems to be the northern terminal of a third stone row which runs tangentially south-west, in the general direction of the stone circle and menhir. In this area are examples of nearly all the prehistoric antiquity types to be found on Dartmoor.

Now head north towards the road, and a cluster of Bronze Age huts will be found. The large, flat, worked stone lying near them owes nothing to prehistoric workmanship, but is a discarded edge-runner from the 19th century, rejected in manufacture. The route back is downhill beside the road to the bridge. On the way you will see another T/A stone 15yd uphill from where the left-hand wall meets the road. Merrivale quarry was begun in 1876, and, not having a rail link, all stone had to be got off Dartmoor by wagons and later by steam traction engines.

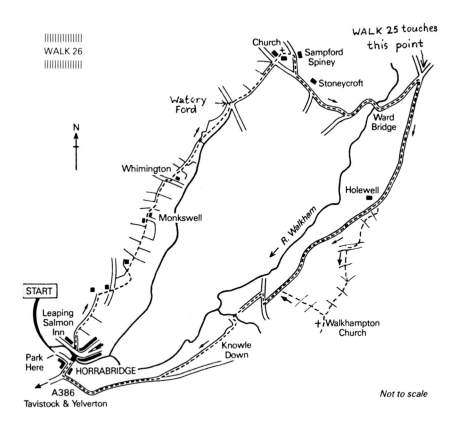

||||||||||||||
WALK 26
||||||||||||||

WALK 25 touches
this point

Church
Sampford
Spiney

Stoneycroft

Watery
Ford

Ward
Bridge

N

Holewell

Whimington

Monkswell

R. Walkham

START

Walkhampton
Church

Leaping
Salmon
Inn

Knowle
Down

Park
Here

HORRABRIDGE

A386
Tavistock & Yelverton

Not to scale

HORRABRIDGE TO SAMPFORD SPINEY AND WALKHAMPTON

WALK 26

★

6½ miles (10.5km)

Dartmoor Outdoor Leisure Map (Ordnance Survey)

This walk is on paths, tracks and quiet country roads. There is one steep climb.
Leave your car in a side road at Horrabridge. The main thoroughfares in Horrabridge are narrow and busy, so avoid causing an obstruction. The village is just off the A386 Yelverton to Tavistock road.
Horrabridge has greatly expanded in recent years, but its centre is attractive and is designated a conservation area. The name puzzles everyone who visits it, and numerous derivations have been suggested. The bridge stands on the boundary between the parishes of Buckland Monachorum and Whitchurch and includes a stone in its structure bearing an incised Latin cross, the actual boundary stone. An old word for boundary is 'har', so 'boundary bridge' has the merit of logicality. (Grid reference: 512 699.)

Leave the village by taking the signposted path which goes up from the car park of the Leaping Salmon Inn. It starts as a narrow lane, but soon enters a field, at the top of which is a stile. Keep the hedge on your left, and pass through a gap into a field containing some large oak trees. Stay by the left hedge for 80yd or so, then make for the gate in the middle of the top fence and turn right along a farm track to the road.
Go up the road for 20yd, then turn right over a stile. Follow the well-marked track across the field. Walkhampton church shows up across the valley, detached by ½ mile from its village, but serving an enormous parish extending up to the neighbourhood of Princetown. We will visit the church on the return route.
Turn left by a low stone building and then right. After passing Monkswell House enter the right gate of two, and keep the hedge on your left, then go along a lane. You pass through Monkswell farm and stay on a track which hugs a hedge at the top of two fields. Descend to the road, climb the stile opposite, and enter the grounds of Whimington, an attractive and interesting old house.
Go to the left of the house and round the back. Enter an ancient lane which gives way to the top of a steep field. Keep the hedge on your left, descend to a stream and climb a step stile tucked away behind a holly tree. After the step stile climb a few yards and bear right to a gate in a

83

fence. Now follow old cart tracks to a stile beside a gate which gets you out onto the road at Watery Ford.

Cross the road, climb a ladder stile beside the green gate. A service reservoir is on your left. Now keep the hedge on your right and make for Sampford Spiney church tower which is visible ahead. Leave the field by a gate at the foot of the village green, but before doing so look out for a fine length of wall just before the gate is reached.

Sampford Spiney is a very atmospheric place; it is hardly a village. Sampford Manor is a well-built house in the vernacular tradition, and on the green are the old school and a tall slender cross. Once it stood in the hedge nearby, but a 19th century Lord of the Manor had it erected in its present more exalted position.

The church has a typical west Dartmoor type tower with large crocketed pinnacles. On the north side of the church is a forbidding stone mausoleum belonging to the Godden family. Peer through the grill in the door, I dare you!

Leave the churchyard by the south-east gate (one can always work out points of the compass by looking at the orientation of a church; the altar is at the east end) and go south along this quiet road towards some stately beech trees.

Just past a large house called Stoneycroft turn left down an unmade road which comes out on a tarmac road by a cattle grid. Continue downhill, and just before a hairpin bend you will notice a stone on the right of the road bearing an incised 'C'. This marked the limit of 'county' responsibility outward from what was a county bridge, Ward Bridge. The present structure replaced an older one which was swept away in a flood in July 1890. The 'C' stone on the south side of the river Walkham seems to have disappeared.

Now climb steeply to the crossroads (the south-west corner of Walk 25 touches this point) and here you turn right — signposted to Walkhampton. Ignore an upward-trending left turn after ¾ mile, but 1 mile from the crossroads, opposite the turning to Holewell farm (right) climb the ladder stile on the south side of the road, to take the Church Path towards Walkhampton church. (If time presses or you are tired this diversion can be classed as optional. The routes link up further on.) This next stretch is well marked with yellow paint blobs and signposts.

Having got into the field, follow the bottom hedge for 80yd. Turn up the next field at 45 degrees to the bottom hedge and after another 80yd climb a stone step stile. Now head for a prominent yellow blob beside the top hedge about 150yd away. There is a stone slab stile here. Climb over it into an old lane. This is the first of several stone stiles, which although simple, are of an unusual sophistication as they exhibit tongue and groove workmanship.

Turn right along the lane for 100yd, and mount a second slab stile left. Here follow the direction indicated by a signpost which is to make for the far top corner of the second field where a yellow blob winks invitingly. Climb a stone step stile and make for the far corner of the field where you should cross a third slab stile. Now follow the hedge, cross the facing bank, and hug the hedge beyond which will bring you to the lane near the Church House.

Turn left and enter the churchyard just past the 16th century Church House. As you pass, look at its interesting south wall. The blocked Tudor doorway must once have been reached by an external stair.

In the churchyard the slate headstones are worth seeing, and a sad memorial near the tower to George Grey who died in 1843 aged 8 'who being placed in charge of some horses lost his way in a fog on Dartmoor and after wandering for two days was found in a state of exhaustion and died soon afterwards'. The story was adapted by Alec Lea into a novel called *To Sunset and Beyond* (Hamish Hamilton 1970).

Now return to the Church House, and pass north down the hill to rejoin the lane you left to walk the Church Path. Cross a stile into a field and make for a stone slab stile in the bottom corner. Then a wooden stile and stone steps leads down into an old lane heading downhill. This lane reaches the road where you should turn left, and right at the next junction signposted to Sampford Spiney.

After descending for 100yd turn left along a track. Near the bottom it can be wet after rain, and there are stepping stones over a small stream. The track veers left round some trees and follows the bottom boundary of this patch of open land, Knowle Down, to the road near the outskirts of Horrabridge. A stroll of about ⅓ mile brings you back to the centre of the village.

As you walk along, a short distance past Horrabridge Primary School, on the right of the road, and opposite Fillace Park, note the newish house called, appropriately, Tinners' Mill. You will see a fine collection of mortar stones and other artefacts in the front garden and drive approach. These were uncovered during a rescue dig before the house was built.

LOWER WALKHAM VALLEY AND DOUBLE WATERS

WALK 27

★

4 miles (6.5km)

Dartmoor Outdoor Leisure Map (Ordnance Survey) — part only
Ordnance Survey Pathfinder Map — Sheet 1340

After a steep initial climb through woodland this walk is not strenuous. The route is entirely on tracks and paths.

Leave your car at Grenofen Bridge, which is reached by turning west off the A386 Tavistock to Yelverton road at the Halfway House Inn. After making the turn, take the first left down a steep lane. Park among the trees on the south side of the bridge. (Grid reference: 490 709.)

From the car park, walk south up the steep winding track through the woods. This is obviously an old road, deep cut as it is and leading down to an ancient crossing place over the river. It was in fact the original road between Buckland Monachorum and Tavistock, both of which had abbeys in pre-dissolution days. The wood is called Sticklepath Wood; 'stickle' means steep, which is very apt.

When the path leaves the woods it levels out, with branches to left and right. These should be ignored, as the correct route is straight ahead along a grassy track used by riders, with tall gorse bushes on both sides and thorn trees scattered about. This is the northern tip of Roborough Down, which extends 5 miles south to the outskirts of Plymouth, but it isn't much visited round here.

When you reach a space at the end used as a car park, turn right down a track marked 'No vehicles beyond this point, except those holding common rights'. A splendid view faces you. The open land opposite is West Down.

The tarred road ends at the entrance to Bucktor, but continue along the track. Notice water flowing out of an old mine adit left. You will see a footbridge over the Walkham, but don't cross it now. Carry on along the track which bears round to the left.

You are at Double Waters, the meeting place of the rivers Walkham and Tavy. Keep on the track until it begins to climb steadily. Leave it here and walk to the river bank. The house perched on a prominent bluff was the mine captain's house of the Virtuous Lady Mine, and the heaps of rubble lying about among the scattered ruins are connected with the mine (copper). It is thought that the mine is old enough to have been called after Queen Elizabeth I.

Walk back up the river along the bank, cross the footbridge, go round

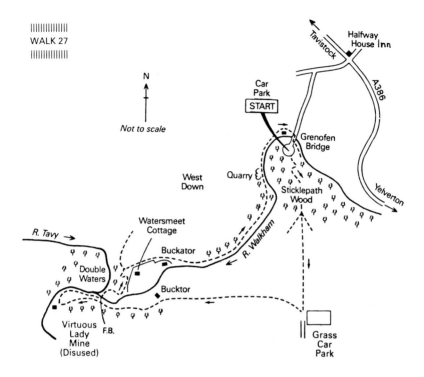

the back of the crag facing you and through the narrow defile on its other side, then up the north bank of the Walkham. The path bends away from the river and climbs past Watersmeet Cottage to a zigzag. Where a rough track comes up right, descend along it, past Buckator (note similar name to the house opposite; I expect they get their letters muddled) and back down to the Walkham.

There is now a very pleasant 1 mile stroll up river, with no impediments to straightforward walking. Just past a large crag to the left you will see some mine buildings, and 300yd further on a walled-up section conceals quarries in the hillside behind. Here the local stone, elvan, was taken out.

As you approach Lower Grenofen House the path conducts you behind the private grounds, then back to the approach drive which leads directly to Grenofen Bridge. Pause on the bridge to see the trout, and possibly salmon, swimming in the deep pool below.

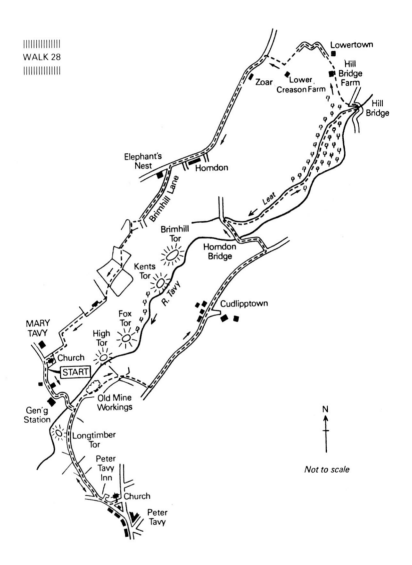

WALK 28

Lowertown

Hill
Bridge
Farm

Zoar

Lower
Creason Farm

Hill
Bridge

Elephant's
Nest

Horndon

Leat

Brimhill Lane

Brimhill
Tor

Horndon
Bridge

Kents
Tor

R. Tavy

Cudlipptown

MARY
TAVY

Fox
Tor

High
Tor

Church

START

N

Old Mine
Workings

Gen'g
Station

Longtimber
Tor

Peter
Tavy
Inn

Church

Not to scale

Peter
Tavy

MARY TAVY, PETER TAVY AND THE TAVY VALLEY

WALK 28

★

6½ miles (10.5km)

Dartmoor Outdoor Leisure Map (Ordnance Survey)

This is a not-too-strenuous walk, but with a probability of mud near the end. The Peter Tavy Inn is seen early in the walk, and the Elephant's Nest Inn towards the end.

There is plenty of space to leave your car in the road outside Mary Tavy church, which is reached by turning east off the A386 Tavistock–Okehampton road. (Grid reference: 509 788.)

Walk down to the footbridge over the river Tavy past the National Power generating station, the large factory-type building on your right. This is a hydro-electric station whose turbines are run by water brought along converted mine leats. You will follow one of these later in the walk.

Once over the footbridge turn right, and follow the path past the lonely Longtimber Tor (right) to Peter Tavy. Dartmoor tors come in all shapes, sizes and situation, and this is one of the most attractive; a mass of trees and rocks.

Peter Tavy church is worth visiting, without having any really special features. Have a look round the village which possesses some pleasant cottages. The Peter Tavy Inn is perhaps the most interesting building in the village, and not only for its structural characteristics!

Now return to the footbridge and take the path which appears to go upstream. After 50yd, on either side of a stile, are two mine adits on the right, one quite large. Once over the stile you will notice a hefty turbine bed at the foot of a pipe. These remains belong to the Devon United Mine, and tin, copper and arsenic were extracted as recently as early last century. Follow the yellow waymarks and at the top of the pipe contour left along the upper limit of the mine workings, and pick up a cart track, the old mine road, which will get you out to the road at a signposted gate. On the way you will see more riverside tors lining the far bank of the Tavy — see map.

Turn left and walk along this quiet road for about 1 mile. You pass through the pretty hamlet of Cudlipptown, and 500yd beyond take the steep rough lane left, but notice the 5ft 6in stone direction post on the corner. A hundred years or so ago signposts were made to last.

Cross the Tavy by Horndon Bridge, ascend the hill beyond and turn right at a stile beside the leat. This is one of the two water supplies for the power station. The other takes its water from the river in Tavy Cleave, several miles up-river.

You now follow the leat for ¾ mile, walking against the direction of flow. Look out for fish darting away as you approach. In places old tramway lines have been pressed into service as fences or stiles. The skill of the hydraulic engineers who planned these leats can only be marvelled at when you see the way this one has been blasted out of the hill.

This waterside stroll comes to an end at Hill Bridge, the take-off point of the leat, where you climb to the road up a nine-rung iron ladder. Notice the perforations in the bridge parapets to allow the free flow of flood water.

Turn left uphill, and enter the gate marked Hill Bridge farm. The building just inside the gate, now a dwelling, was once a small local school. From here follow the track past the farm, a riding establishment, and Lowertown, a white-painted house. Beyond here the route zigzags and comes out on open land near the entrance to Lower Creason farm. Turn right here, and left at the road.

Now keep on the road past the hamlets of Zoar and Horndon to the pub called the Elephant's Nest. The sharply-pointed hill in the distance is Brent Tor, with a small church on its summit, and even a tiny burial ground.

This area has a very Cornish flavour, due to the cottages being built in the Cornish tradition by the miners who came here to exploit Dartmoor's minerals. Horndon had two places of worship, a Methodist chapel (1904) with a neighbouring Chile pine (monkey puzzle tree); and an Anglican church (1860) with a bell turret. It hasn't been used since 1960, but can't be sold as the deeds are lost. It is now used as a barn.

Go down Brimhill Lane behind the Elephant's Nest car park. When the lane bears left at the power station header-pond, climb the stone step stile and make for the nearest wall corner facing you 50yd away. Here is another step stile. Scale it, and turn left along a short lane. Enter a field and follow the right-hand hedge, making for a gate. Bear half left here and head for a corner where there is another step stile. Now follow the hedge facing you to yet another step stile in the corner. Bear half left again and make for the field corner.

Now follow a track, often muddy, past a building with a chimney, and at the bottom of this field, over a ladder stile, you will have a low wall on your left for company. Where this veers left, follow the bottom hedge and turn right at a gate. Now follow the hedge to a step stile which admits you to the top east corner of Mary Tavy churchyard.

Some 15yd south of here is the Gothic-pointed gravestone, somewhat leaning, of Mr and Mrs William Crossing. William Crossing was a notable Dartmoor authority who died in 1928. His *Guide to Dartmoor*, available as a reprint, is esteemed by many as Holy Writ.

Your car is now a few yards away at the foot of the churchyard.

DOE TOR BROOK AND WIDGERY CROSS

WALK 29

★

3 miles (4.8km)

Dartmoor Outdoor Leisure Map (Ordnance Survey)

This is a short and easy open moor walk on north-west Dartmoor. It should not, however, be attempted in mist unless you are accomplished in map and compass work.

Leave your car in the car park beyond the gate at the approach to High Down. This is reached by driving up the rough lane beside the Dartmoor Inn on the A386 Tavistock–Okehampton road, opposite the Lydford turning. (Grid reference: 526 854.)

Walk over High Down along the left-hand wall and down to the river Lyd which is crossed by a footbridge or stepping stones. This spot is interesting as being the exact boundary between the granite (east of the river) and the metamorphic rock.

Turn right along a green path which roughly follows the river which falls away on your right. After 200yd look out for a conspicuous rock on the far bank with a couple of seats nearby. A plaque fixed to the rock — Black Rock — serves as a memorial to a young army officer, killed in France in 1918, who had visited the area shortly before his death.

At the point where the Doe Tor Brook hurries beneath the path, turn up left beside the stream and climb steeply past Doe Tor Falls, a modest cataract. Further up is an area of heaped rubble. This was Foxhole Mine. The actual 'works' were further upstream.

When you reach flattish land at the top of the fast-flowing section you will see a number of red and white poles on your right. These mark the northern boundary of the Willsworthy firing range, and you should on no account pass the line of poles if red flags are flying on high points in the vicinity. However, the route as given does not require you to do so!

Keep on the same bank of the brook and follow it round so that you are heading north, and where the valley begins to narrow you will come across the roofless ruin of the Foxhole Mine building. This is an interesting site. The house has two chimneys and is better preserved than many similar sites. Perhaps this is because it is tucked away and remote from the much-frequented trade routes of potential vandals. They are even present on Dartmoor, I am afraid.

In front of the ruin are the remains of two buddles, circular devices for sorting the tin concentrates after crushing, and to the north is the

91

WALK 29

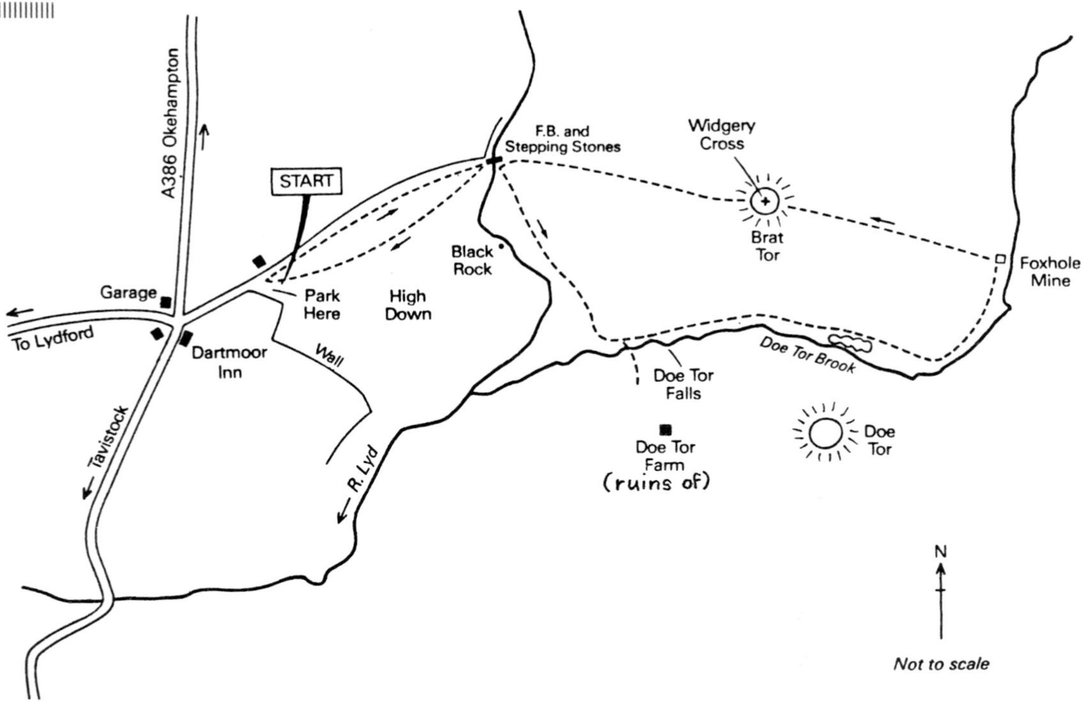

START

Park Here

High Down

Wall

Black Rock

F.B. and Stepping Stones

Widgery Cross

Brat Tor

Foxhole Mine

Doe Tor Brook

Doe Tor Falls

Doe Tor

Doe Tor Farm (ruins of)

R. Lyd

A386 Okehampton

To Lydford

Garage

Dartmoor Inn

Tavistock

N

Not to scale

filled-up wheel pit and tail race with the ramp and leat along which the water was conducted to the wheel.

A well researched three-page illustrated article about the Foxhole Mine complex by Dr Tom Greeves appeared in the *Dartmoor Magazine* No. 73, for winter 2003. Other names for this enterprise were Wheal Frederick, the Duke of Wellington Console, and the North Dartmoor Tin Mining Company. The active years appear to have been between 1845 and 1887.

Now turn your back on the Doe Tor Brook and head westwards to the summit of Brat Tor (sometimes engagingly spelt Bra Tor!) which has a stone cross on its highest point. It is not a single hewn monolith, but an aggregate of built-up blocks constructed to mark Queen Victoria's Silver Jubilee in 1887 on the instruction of Mr William Widgery, a well-known Dartmoor artist.

William Crossing tells the story of Widgery painting on the moor when an acquaintance passed by, looked over his shoulder and failed to recognise the picture being painted from the view before him. In the foreground instead of a marsh there was a rocky stream. 'Mr Widgery', said the visitor mildly, 'there is no river at the foot of that hill.' 'Isn't there?' returned the artist, without looking up. 'Well, there ought to be.' I sometimes wonder if the passer-by was Crossing himself!

Stop here to take in the view. To the west, if the day is clear, Bodmin Moor forms the skyline. At the foot of the tor the Lyd threads its way, and over to the north-west is the rounded hill known as Great Nodden. Look carefully and you will see the line of a long-disused railway curling round its plum-pudding form. This enterprise carried down peat from extensive beds beyond Great Links Tor, the fine feature to the north-east. One of its optimistic promoters even visualised running the British Navy on peat instead of coal.

Now descend the tor to the footbridge, and return to your car across High Down.

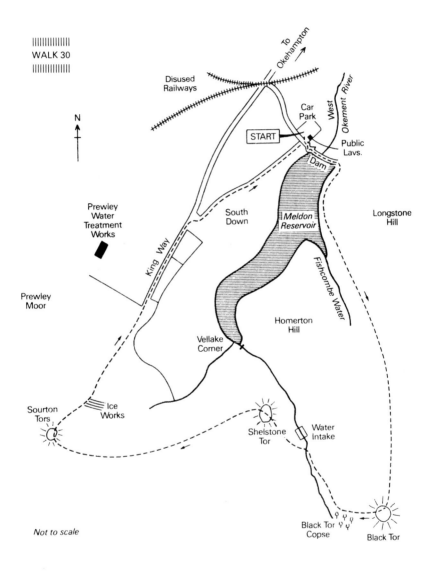

||||||||||||||
WALK 30
||||||||||||||

Disused
Railways

To
Okehampton

West
Okement River

N

Car
Park

START

Public
Lavs.

Dam

Prewley
Water
Treatment
Works

South
Down

Meldon
Reservoir

Longstone
Hill

King Way

Fishcombe Water

Prewley
Moor

Homerton
Hill

Vellake
Corner

Ice
Works

Sourton
Tors

Shelstone
Tor

Water
Intake

Not to scale

Black Tor
Copse

Black Tor

THE MELDON RESERVOIR, WEST OKEMENT VALLEY AND THE SOURTON TORS

WALK 30

★

5 miles (8km)

Dartmoor Outdoor Leisure Map (Ordnance Survey)

This is an open moor walk with some climbing. It should not be attempted in mist unless you are accomplished in map and compass work.

Leave your car in the public car park at Meldon reservoir. There are public lavatories. The car park is 2½ miles south-west of the centre of Okehampton, now bypassed (1988) by the A30 to the south. There is no direct access to Meldon if travelling westwards along this road, but the motorist may carry on to the roundabout at Sourton Cross and then return along the eastbound carriageway, taking the slip road signposted to Meldon. (Grid reference: 562 918.)

From the car park, walk to the far (east) end of the dam and look about you. The reservoir was built between 1970 and 1972 after a protracted argument going back to 1962. Those who knew the valley before cannot agree that the dam has improved the scene. Down the valley is a large quarry where much of the ballast for British Rail originates.

From this end of the dam take the track for 100yd, then bear up left past scattered thorn trees. Once over a rise, aim for the head of a steep narrow valley entering the reservoir from the south. This is the Fishcombe Water. To accomplish this, pick up a sheep path to facilitate progress across the steep slope. You are climbing diagonally across the hill all the time.

Go past a small cascade which is a delightful sequestered corner. Mountain ash and hollies grow here. Follow the tiny stream up trying to stay on dry ground, with the headwater springs to your right.

Keep looking ahead, and when the twin humps of Black Tor come into view, make towards them, then drop steeply downhill to the West Okement river. As you descend you will be just outside the northern limits of Black Tor Copse, one of the three old natural upland oak woods of Dartmoor. The wood is sometimes called Black Tor Beare, which means the same thing; 'beare' is an old name for a wood.

It is thought that many Dartmoor valleys once had similar groves, but Wistmans Wood beside the West Dart river at Two Bridges and Piles Copse up the Erme from Ivybridge are all that remain. Tin miners, fuel scavengers, grazing animals and fire are thought to be responsible for the depletion. For the sites which have survived we can probably thank the rocky slopes out of which they grow, and they are now protected by various official designations.

The West Okement has now to be crossed, and this can often be done by stepping from rock to rock just upstream from the walled water intake 500yd down-river from the north end of the copse. If the river is running high this should not be attempted. There is a footbridge ½ mile downstream at Vellake Corner.

Assuming you have crossed near the intake, climb now to Shelstone Tor, then walk due west across a smooth-turfed bowl to the crested Sourton Tors, 1 mile away on the skyline. As you climb the last 300yd to the tors you will cross the line of an ancient track, the King Way, the original route between Okehampton and Tavistock. (The obvious way up from the footbridge links with the Shelstone Tor route here.)

Having feasted on the view (and the Bristol Channel is sometimes visible) head north-east and aim for a long hedge to the right of the prominent Prewley water treatment works. A little distance down from the summit you will come across five or six long, shallow, grass-grown troughs. They look more like earthworks than anything else. They were so constructed that water would fill them so that ice would form. The ice was collected and hurried down to Plymouth for the fishing industry as required. In the gulley below the lowest trough is all that remains of a subterranean ice house where the ice was stored. This site was chosen as it was elevated, north facing and near to the railway for rapid transmission to Plymouth. A nearby spring provided the water. Even so, it wasn't one of Dartmoor's more successful ventures; most of the ice melted in transit! This site is marked on the 1889 6in map as Ice Ponds, and appears to have been fenced against animals.

Enter a lane — you are now on the King Way — by a line of prominent hedgerow beeches, and carry on along here until, when nearly abreast of the highest part of South Down to the right, a wall faces you. Bear right round the outside of the wall, and don't enter the narrow lane. Keep the hedge on your left and follow it down to the reservoir car park.